O.

HA

1

1

CS

F

ROTATION
PLAN

COURAGE
UNDER FIRE

COMBAT
STRESS

They fight our wars.   We fight their battles.

COURAGE
UNDER FIRE

E&T

First published 2010 by Elliott and Thompson Limited
27 John Street, London WC1N 2BX
www.eandtbooks.com

ISBN: 9781904027959

Design copyright: Elliott & Thompson
Text copyright: Tim Lynch

First published: 2010

9 8 7 6 5 4 3 2 1

A CIP catalogue record for this book is available from the British Library.

Printed and bound in the UK by CPI Mackays, Chatham ME5 8TD

Typeset in Minion and Gill Sans

ACKNOWLEDGEMENTS

'Soldier' reproduced by kind permission of Harvey Andrews
and Westminster Music Ltd
'PTSD' by Jim Love © Jim Love 2010
'No Heroes' by David Morgan DSC

CONTENTS

FOREWORD

Imagine a young man today, going on patrol in Afghanistan, knowing that he will face Improvised Explosive Devices and that the chance of seeing one detonate is statistically very high. He is effectively walking through an unmarked minefield. He will have known, or at least heard of, comrades who will have lost limbs doing so. He will be doing that day in, day out. It is not uncommon to see a soldier vomit through fear when faced with that knowledge, but who is nonetheless able to take his life in his hands and do it anyway.

For me, the notion of 'courage under fire' can be split into two very distinct, but equally vital, parts. Physical courage is perhaps the most often considered form of courage, but moral courage is every bit as important. Under fire, you will behave instinctively. You need physical courage to put yourself in harm's way, but you also need the moral courage to do the right thing, instinctively.

Courage is one of the six core values (outlined on pp. 50-51) the army introduced around ten years ago. It has placed a greater emphasis on the need for moral courage in recent years. Physical courage has always been there, throughout history, and is very likely to remain, as it is not possible to fight wars without it. New service personnel are educated that there is a right thing and a wrong thing to do in any difficult situation and they are trained to choose the right thing, even under enormous pressure. Whether witnessing harassment of a female comrade or of an Iraqi civilian, for example, it takes great moral courage to speak out and stop it. It would be easy for them to do nothing or look the other way, but we should be proud that they do not, whether through this training or their own moral values.

Only a very small percentage of the population has served, or had a family member serve, in the military. Therefore, only a minority of people know first-hand the pressures that servicemen are under. This is why it's more important than ever that the work of charities like Combat Stress is supported by the public. As an entity run specifically for veterans, they understand the behaviour, the language and the needs of servicemen in a way that a public service like the NHS cannot.

There is a greater understanding and acceptance of mental health issues in the Army than ever before. Soldiers are alert to members of their platoon or company who might be showing signs of distress and know how to deal with such signs. The problem can be addressed by getting someone who understands that these things are normal, talking to them, and addressing it very early on.

History shows an unequal balance between civilians and servicemen seeking help. The average time it takes for a serviceman to begin to look for treatment for mental health issues is fourteen years. Indeed, there are Falklands veterans only beginning to ask for support now. As more soldiers return from Iraq and Afghanistan help will be needed for years to come. Donations to charities like Combat Stress make a life-changing difference to these men and women who have risked their lives serving their country. They need all the help we can give them.

General Sir Richard Dannatt GCB CBE MC DL

NO HEROES

There were no heroes here
Amongst the men who tramped through
Rutted, quaking moor,
Or crawled, cat-silent,
Over skittering scree
To prove the way.

No heroes fought the blazing fires
Which sucked the very blood from
Ship and man alike.
Or braved knife cold
Without a thought
To save a life.

No heroes they, but ones who loved
Sweet life and children's laugh,
And dreamt of home
When war allowed.
They were but men.

David Morgan DSC
800 Naval Air Squadron
Falkland Islands Task Force 1982

INTRODUCTION

There are no heroes in Afghanistan.

It's not a word soldiers use about themselves. In the midst of a firefight, when the lives of your mates depend on your next move, two things – heroics and hysterics – will get you all killed. What matters most as the rounds come in is the ability to remember your training and do what has to be done. Medals are won in a few short minutes; wars are won by enduring day after endless day. It is in the long, grinding routine of fear, exhaustion and hunger that a soldier's worth is measured and his true character revealed. To be called a hero by the press at home means nothing. To be called a good soldier by friends who have seen you at your best and at your worst is beyond price.

Navy Medical Assistant Kate Nesbitt was on her first tour of duty in Afghanistan, working as a patrol medic attached to the 1st Battalion, The Rifles when, as she later remembered, 'Without warning Taliban fighters opened fire, having ambushed us. Within seconds I heard, 'Man down, man down,' on the radio and I knew I was needed. I got the location details and sprinted towards him while under fire. All I was thinking was,

'There's a casualty and I need to be there'. I just thought the quicker I get to him the more chance I have to save his life. It was adrenalin. Whenever I went on patrol I hoped I wouldn't be needed – but when the call came I knew I had to step up to the mark.'

After crossing 70m of open ground to reach Corporal John List, she found him choking to death on his own blood. 'When I first got there I didn't think he was going to make it. He was struggling to breathe and I had to provide him with another airway. The round had gone through his top lip, ruptured his jaw and come out of his neck. He was so lucky it didn't hit an artery.' Nesbitt worked for 45 minutes to stabilise List's injuries before he could be evacuated to hospital, working continuously with heavy fire all around her.

Her actions that day won her the Military Cross with a citation that read, 'Her actions throughout a series of offensive operations were exemplary; under fire and under pressure her commitment and courage were inspirational and made the difference between life and death. She performed in the highest traditions of her service.' When she received the award, Nesbitt told reporters that 'being described as a hero is just too much. I did my job the best I could. It was just overwhelming to hear people say 'well done' and that he made it through.' The praise was nice, but I would have been over the moon with a good [appraisal] report.'

Iain McRobbie survived the sinking of HMS *Ardent* during the Falklands War and recalls returning to a hero's welcome. 'I could have done without that, actually. "Hero" is a word that is used far too often. I was doing the job I was paid to do – it's not something I would like to have to do again. To me, the heroes are the guys whose names are on all these cenotaphs all over Britain. The country is full of people who have done things like that – squaddies who served in Northern Ireland, old men who were at Monte Cassino.' It was a sentiment echoed years later by 18-year-old Alex Kennedy, who won the Military Cross after only eight months in the army during his first tour of Afghanistan. He insisted, 'I don't feel like a hero – that title should really go to those who go out to

Afghanistan and don't make it back.' No veteran, it seems, ever claims to be a hero, but every one of them knows someone else who was.

Journalists, though, like the word. To them it can mean someone who rescues a cat from a tree or a child from a blazing house. It can mean a highly paid sportsman who wins a game and finally earns his enormous salary, or it can mean the milkman who carried out his rounds when it snowed. It can mean whatever they choose it to mean. To the journalist, any soldier in wartime becomes a hero and any ex-serviceman with a campaign medal automatically becomes a 'decorated war hero' until the term is cheapened by casual use. Certainly, none of the veterans whose stories appear here would thank you for calling them heroic. Time and again, the common thread that links those whose outstanding bravery has earned them recognition is one of humility and embarrassment for being singled out for doing what they insist anyone would have done in their place.

The medals won by Kate and Alex were richly deserved. Medals are the visible means by which society measures and rewards bravery, though every holder of a gallantry award knows that they are only the tip of the iceberg. A hundred medals a day are being earned in Afghanistan as I write, but only a very few will ever be presented. For most of those who serve, the sole recognition for the months during which they survived daily firefights and terrors we at home could never dream of will be a campaign medal. Outwardly dismissed as the medal equivalent of haemorrhoids ('any arsehole can get them') and claimed by the rough, tough, world-weary and cynical recipients to be awards that are handed out with the rations, they are, nevertheless, secretly treasured as evidence that the wearer was there. Medal holders belong to an exclusive group, in Shakespeare's words: 'we few, we happy few, we band of brothers'. 'A soldier will fight long and hard for a bit of coloured ribbon,' wrote Napoleon Bonaparte, knowing that for the men who have earned the right to wear that coloured ribbon, it will forever be a bond between them that sets them apart from other men. Most people at home tend to think of courage under fire only in terms of elite units and the presentation of medals for outstanding acts of heroism, but the unglamorous former army truck driver wearing a row of campaign medals whose memoirs will never be published may have spent far more time working under enemy fire than the commando with a gallantry award. Only the person wearing medals can ever really know what it took to win them.

In preparing this book I spoke to many veterans and I asked one, a former Special Forces soldier who had served with distinction in the Gulf, what he thought a book like this should be about. At a time when the British public is showing ever more support for their troops, what should I tell them about courage under fire? 'Tell them the truth,' he replied. 'Tell them it's nothing like they see on telly. Tell them that when those lads come back and the charity buckets disappear, they'll still be fighting the war – day in, day out, night in, night out – until they get the help they deserve.'

This, then, is not a book about heroes, but one about courage under fire and what this means. It is not a catalogue of stirring deeds by an elite soldier whose adventures are described in action-packed bestsellers – men who fearlessly face the enemy with a stiff upper lip and a reckless disregard for danger. The tiny, unimaginative minority who truly are fearless have no need of courage. 'An awful lot is talked about bravery,' one World War II veteran said, 'but I think there's a hell of a difference between being brave and being fearless. People are fearless because they don't feel any fear. People who are brave are probably shit-scared at the time but manage to do great things. There were one or two people I met who appeared to be fearless. Whether they were very intelligent or very sick, I don't know. They had a very different outlook. Maybe they had no imagination? I don't know if you should envy the fearless chap.'

Genuine courage comes from those who know what risks lay ahead, feel real fear, yet act anyway because it seems the right thing to do. Courage is not found with the John Waynes and Rambos of the world, but in the teenager who is terrified to the point of soiling himself but who goes on anyway because that is what has been asked of him. Former tennis champion and political activist Arthur Ashe once claimed that 'true heroism is remarkably sober, very undramatic. It is not the urge to surpass all others at whatever cost, but the urge to serve others at whatever cost.' The stories in this book show how the British military's reputation for determination and professionalism is founded in a million everyday acts of quiet, undramatic courage by men and women who believe that there are some things more important than themselves. Greatest of all these is the belief in the value of friendship. Rarely do soldiers fight and die for abstract causes. Few offer their lives for their country and its flag – but a great many have died for their friends. It is a measure of our society and the men and women who represent it that in any military operation, far more medals are awarded for saving lives than for taking them.

Without exception, the men and women who risk everything in the service of others are quick to dismiss any suggestion that they are somehow special. 'I'm no hero,' they say, 'I was just doing my job.' This is a book about that job. It shows how ordinary people face an extraordinary experience. At a time when young people are viewed with suspicion by the media and by their own communities, here is what ordinary young people are capable of.

The stories that follow are heavily slanted towards the experiences of soldiers. No slight is intended towards the contribution of other services – few of us who landed on the islands in the Falklands War envied our naval colleagues aboard ships which seemed little more than sitting targets as they rode at anchor, inviting attack, to draw the bombs away from the troopships. No one who lived through the Blitz could criticise the willingness of the young RAF pilots who, several times a day, rose to meet the seemingly unstoppable aerial armada intent on bombing Britain into submission. In an age of intercontinental missiles and laser-guided bombs, it is still the soldier on the ground with rifle and bayonet who takes and holds ground. 'Let us be clear about three facts,' wrote Field-Marshal Earl Wavell in 1945. 'First, all battles and all wars are won in the end by the infantryman. Secondly, the infantryman always bears the brunt. His casualties are heavier, he suffers greater extremes of discomfort and fatigue than the other arms. Thirdly, the art of the infantryman is less stereotyped and far harder to acquire in modern war than that of any other arm … The infantryman has to use initiative and intelligence in almost every step he moves, every action he takes on the battlefield.'

Whatever the advances in weapons technology and tactics, the soldier's existence today would broadly be recognisable to the veterans of Normandy, of the Somme, of Waterloo. The endless slogging along with rifle and pack; the cold, lonely vigil of the sentry at night; the misery; the hunger; the exhaustion; the comradeship; the terror and exhilaration of being under fire; the joy at survival; the dream of home.

Soldiers live in a world that the families and friends they leave behind can only begin to imagine. It's a world of emotional highs and lows which can turn an idealistic teenager old and cynical in a matter of weeks, but even at its worst is still a world they would never want to forget. No matter how old the veteran, the memories of military service remain fresh in later years as they gather in ever dwindling bands of survivors to remember those they once marched beside. Each November at memorials around the country, for a little while they walk taller, straighter and with a sense of pride, remembering their lost youth and the friends they knew – young men who laughed and drank together, shared their hopes and dreams but who never came back. The veterans go home to a life that somehow never quite lived up to what they once dreamed it would be. A soldier who served in Vietnam summed up the quandary every veteran faces at some point: 'Sometimes I wish I could be back there, just for a little while, just so I could wish I was back here.'

For those who survive, no war ends when the last bullet is fired. For good, for bad, war changes those who see it at close quarters. This is not merely a book about where courage under fire comes from – it is also about what that courage costs. We frequently hear our politicians speak of the debt we owe to our armed forces, but few of us know what that really means. Servicemen and women are told that their sacrifice will never be forgotten, but it too often is as we go about the safe, comfortable routine of our daily lives. Here, in their own words, are the voices of those to whom the debt is owed. Here is why we owe them a duty to remember what we once asked them to do.

CHAPTER ONE
THE MILITARY

The army sleep under the stars. The navy navigates by the stars. The RAF books into hotels using the stars.

Graffiti in a British base, Basra

People often talk about the military as a family, which is a good analogy. There are three siblings who, even if they squabble among themselves, will always help each other against outsiders.

Eldest of the three is the Royal Navy, founded in the reign of Henry VIII as the Navy Royal, Britain's first full-time standing military force. As an island state, Britain depended on the English Channel to defend it against foreign threat, but it also needed to ensure the safety of its trading fleets. The existence of the navy was seen as vital to the country's survival. Not that that gave it much status. Writing in the eighteenth century, Samuel Johnson claimed that 'no man will be a sailor who has contrivance enough to get himself into a jail; for being in a ship is being in jail with the chance of being drowned'. So poor were the pay and conditions that by the time of Trafalgar, around five in every six men serving in the navy had been forcibly conscripted by the notorious press gangs who roamed the coastal ports and harbours abducting any man deemed fit to sail.

Things changed during Queen Victoria's reign. The growth of the Empire and the expansion of foreign trade made it vital that Britannia should rule the waves. It was an era of gunboat diplomacy in which the Royal Navy imposed peace through the superior firepower of the world's largest fleet. Technological advances made the old, labour-intensive sailing ships a thing of the past and recruits were now needed for smaller, more skilled, crews. Consequently, from the middle of the nineteenth century, better pay, uniforms, conditions and terms of service began to make a career in the navy an attractive prospect, especially since at the same time the public perception of the navy became increasingly positive: Nelson had become a cult figure and Trafalgar Day was widely celebrated across the Empire in parades, dinners and other events. In newspapers, books, plays and songs the image of the 'Jolly Jack Tar' had become well established as the man who made Britain great. By the turn of the twentieth century, music-hall crowds happily sang along as entertainers sang 'All the nice girls love a sailor ...' and even that great champion of the common soldier, Rudyard Kipling, argued in a school textbook of 1911 that 'to serve King and Country in the Army is the second best profession for Englishmen of all classes; to serve in the Navy, I suppose we all admit, is the best'.

The Royal Air Force is the baby of the family. Formed as the world's first independent air force in 1918 (on April Fool's Day, as their colleagues in other services gleefully point out), from the outset the RAF enjoyed an exciting reputation. In 1918, four years of muddy stalemate were coming to an end. In sharp contrast to the filthy infantryman far below, the aviator was seen as a romantic figure, a true 'knight of the air' fighting chivalrous duels in the sky, one man against another in a new and glamorous type of warfare.

In the years following World War I, the belief grew that 'the bomber will always get through'. Strategic bombing, it was thought, would be a war-winning weapon. No longer was the English Channel enough – bombers would be able to cross it in minutes from airfields in France and Belgium. The navy might be Britain's first line of defence, but aircraft would come a close second. In 1940 the RAF achieved its greatest success by holding back the Luftwaffe in a battle against the odds that has become a symbol of all that is considered best about Britain. In the popular imagination, the RAF is still the home of dashing young men from good schools who work far from the squalid reality of war in the world of the top guns.

And in between is the army. Not royal, not senior, not popular, but the classic example of the middle child. It's said that the middle child is constantly reminded of the achievements of its elder and younger siblings but always missing out on attention for itself until it feels like an outsider in the family. For most of its existence, the army has indeed been treated as very much the outsider.

From Anglo Saxon times, every man had been expected to be available to defend his homeland. By the Middle Ages, Posse Comitatus required the Shire Reeve (or Sheriff) of a county to keep a register of men he could call upon in the event of attack or civil emergency. The Act was passed into US law in 1871 and led to the Sheriff's Posse of western fame. Forced service in times of crisis, though, was widely seen as a due that had to be paid, however unpopular it might be. When Civil War broke out in England in 1642, both sides used Posse Comitatus to conscript every able-bodied man they could find. They were expected to fight far beyond the borders of their home county, seen by critics as a breach of the unspoken rule of service only to defend one's home, which cast a long shadow across the army and the society it serves. In the series of battles that rocked the country between 1642 and 1651 it has been estimated that around a quarter of the male population of Britain was coerced into military service at some point and, of those conscripted, a conservative estimate of around 190,000 are believed to have died as a result of wounds or disease directly linked to their service – 3.7 per cent of the population of England and Wales. In Scotland, 6 per cent died and in Ireland 41 per cent, leaving a bitter legacy. By comparison, the slaughter of World War I cost Britain as a whole 1.53 per cent of its population.

With the end of the Civil War came the start of a military dictatorship under Cromwell's Protectorate that placed zealous Puritan generals in control of the counties of England and Wales. Though brief, the memory of their rule has traditionally been remembered as one of tyrannical despots ruling over their regions with an iron fist, crushing any vestige of royalist support and imposing fanatical religious ideology on the masses. 'Unfortunately,' wrote Kipling in his history of Britain, 'this reign of the Sword left on Men's minds an unreasonable hatred and fear, not only of this Puritan army, but of all armies, and that hatred and fear has too often paralysed the arm of England, and is not wholly dead today.'

The restoration of the monarchy in 1660 came at a time when distrust of the power of the army was at its height. Charles II disbanded it entirely only to immediately face the threat of rebellion, which forced him to review the decision. Four regiments – two of infantry, two of cavalry – would be retained as a personal security force for the King's Household. The modern British army was born but it would be almost a century before the force was recognised as an army, Parliament referring only to 'our guards and garrisons' in its annual defence spending estimates until the mid-eighteenth century. Fear of any future attempt by the army to overthrow the government and king meant that measures had been put in place to prevent it becoming too powerful. Its appointed officers were men selected for their vested interest in maintaining the status quo and conditions for the lower ranks kept poor to ensure that it attracted only men who lacked ambition. Enlistment was for life and discipline sometimes fatally harsh.

Alone among the European powers, the shadow of the Civil War losses meant Britain remained determined to avoid the need to introduce conscription. Where other countries faced the threat of land invasion,

Britain relied on its naval power to ensure that no other navy could reach its shores. Its army was, by and large, an expeditionary force to be transported by the navy to wherever it was needed abroad. Its sole purpose was to enforce British might and its men did not need to be bright, the government demanded, just cheap and disposable. Quality was unimportant. The Duke of Wellington campaigned for a form of National Service, arguing that in other countries generals had men of every class and rank among their troops, bringing intelligence and initiative to even the newest recruit, whilst the British, he said, made do with an army 'composed of the scum of the earth – the mere scum of the earth. It is only wonderful that we should be able to make so much out of them afterwards.'

And scum they were. By the time of Waterloo the army had earned a reputation as the last refuge for rogues, drunkards and ne'er-do-wells. They were men who had frequently faced the choice to serve in the army or be sent to prison, men who would not be missed if anything should happen to them. In the years following Wellington's great victory, 'Waterloo Teeth' became a fashionable item among the wealthy. As the corpses cooled on the battlefield, they were stripped of their weapons, valuables, clothing and equipment. Then came men with pliers to pull out their teeth to make high-class dentures. Finally, long after the celebrations had ended, the fallen heroes of Waterloo came home – their ground-up bones transported in barrels as cheap fertilizer, such was the lack of esteem for the fallen soldiers.

Forty years later, another war was under way. In 1853 British troops were sent to the Crimea as part of an alliance that also included French, Turkish, Sardinian and German troops attempting to block the expansion of the Russian Empire. It was to become a campaign famous for its catastrophic failures, but one which would also see tremendous feats of courage and endurance. One action, above all others, became a legend.

Just after 11.00am on 25 October 1854, James Thomas Brudenell, the 7th Lord Cardigan, received orders from the army commander that the

670 men under his command were 'to advance rapidly to the front, follow the enemy, and try to prevent the enemy carrying away the guns'. The message ended with a terse 'Immediate'.

The order referred to naval artillery being moved from a British redoubt captured by the Russians on a hill nearby. From where he sat, Cardigan could see only one set of guns, at the far end of the valley between the Fedyukhin Heights and the Causeway Heights. Ahead of him were around fifty artillery pieces and twenty battalions of Russian troops spread along the high ground on each side. The orders were suicidal and Cardigan knew it, but when he asked for clarification, he was again ordered to advance.

With little choice but to obey, Cardigan gave the order to 'Draw Swords'. Then he led his men forward, swords and lances held upright, pennons snapping in the breeze. Private Robert Farquharson overheard someone comment that many of them would not be returning from this attack. Private William Pennington recalled that he 'had no hope of life'. 'Every private soldier could see what a mistake was being made,' wrote Private John Richardson of the 11th Hussars, 'but all we had to do was obey orders.'

Then, at 11.10am, Cardigan gave his second order: 'The brigade will advance. First squadron of the 17th Lancers direct.' Beside him, Bugler Billy Brittain of the 17th sounded the command, 'Walk'. As the brigade moved forward, Cardigan said quietly, 'Here goes the last of the Brudenells.'

As the brigade opened up into attack formation, Cardigan gave the order, 'Trot'. The horses increased their speed to the textbook eight and a half miles per hour. They would move at this speed until they were 250 yards from their objective before launching into a gallop. The final, headlong charge would begin just forty yards from the enemy. Across the lines, the men were silent. Experienced cavalrymen knew that it would take seven minutes to reach the enemy guns – but seven minutes is a long time under fire.

At 11.11am the first Russian guns opened up from a battery on the brigade's left flank. Almost immediately Captain Nolan, the man who had brought the order and who many would later blame for misdirecting Cardigan, was killed. 'I shall never forget the shriek that he gave,' said Private Henry Naylor of the 13th Dragoons, 'it rung in my ears above the roaring of the cannon.' As the brigade advanced, the Russian fire seemed directed only at Cardigan, riding ahead of his men. The first crashing volley was followed by an ominous silence as the gunners reloaded.

From their vantage point high on the nearby hills, the British commander Lord Raglan and his staff watched the brigade move forward and gasped in horror as, instead of turning towards the Causeway Heights redoubt as expected, they instead trotted straight forward. Then came the second volley.

As enemy cannonballs ripped into the riders, some attempted to quicken the pace. Then, at 11.15, the guns on the right flank also opened up. Still the brigade moved forward at a steady trot with Cardigan setting the pace. Around them, the cavalrymen saw their comrades blasted to pieces. James Wightman watched the headless body of his troop sergeant ride on for thirty yards before tumbling to the ground. William Pennington recalled a man's forearm hanging by its tendons and 'brains protruding from a shattered skull'. Around them, the volume of fire increased as enemy infantrymen joined in with volleys of musketry. Still they trotted.

By now the leading line was about halfway down the valley and under fire from both flanks. Wightman felt a twitch on his arm. Beside him his friend John Lee had been 'all but smashed by a shell'. With a strange smile, Lee bid him goodbye and fell out of the saddle, his horse keeping pace as her entrails fell from her. Men who had been wounded clung to their saddles and pressed on, knowing that Russian sharpshooters would soon pick off stragglers. Men whose horses were killed were also at risk, their only hope to mount a riderless horse and catch up with their units. Still the brigade kept the same pace.

At 11.16, the remaining riders had advanced to within 250 yards of the guns and Cardigan ordered the gallop. Ahead, the line of Russian guns directly in front of them began to load canister rounds – a packed container of small balls making the cannons into deadly shotguns. Some used double loads of a cannonball and a canister round to maximise the damage they could do at close quarters. Captain Godfrey Morgan was close enough to see the gunner light the fuse of one gun. 'I shut my eyes for I thought that settled the question as far as I was concerned, but the shot missed me and struck the man on my right full on the chest.'

At last, Cardigan shouted 'Charge!' but few could have heard it. Along the line, lances were lowered as the remaining horsemen smashed into the eight Russian guns positioned at the head of the valley, hacking down the crews as they finally struck home. Their desperate momentum carried the Lancers through the gun lines and into a thick cloud of smoke that hung over the Russian battery. When Captain Morris of the 17th Lancers pulled his horse to a halt, he found just twenty men still with him from the regiment he had led into action seven minutes before. Worse, as the smoke thinned, he saw a complete regiment of Russian Hussars waiting for him.

Their orders had been to prevent the Russians carrying off the guns but the survivors of the charge now knew that whether or not they attempted to retrieve the guns, the massed Russian cavalry would slaughter them as they withdrew down the valley. Their only hope lay in attack. In the confusion, Colonel Mayow, the brigade's second in command, attempted to rally what men he could – just fifteen Lancers and twelve Dragoons.

The Russian cavalry had lined up about 100 yards behind the guns and, believing that no one could survive the firepower they had faced, were as surprised to see the British emerge from the smoke as the British were to see the Russian cavalry waiting for them. Morris seized the initiative and immediately plunged his small force directly into the enemy. The shock of an attack by this small band of apparent madmen created a psychological impact out of all proportion to the size of the force. The Russians scattered.

Nearby, Colonel Mayow also led his 27 men directly into the front ranks of a massed Cossack cavalry regiment. Even though they had watched the charge and knew that there would be no reinforcements to support this tiny force, the Cossacks fled the furious onslaught.

But not all the Russians fled. As the bands of British cavalrymen gathered at the head of the valley, it became clear that Russian Lancers had positioned themselves along the heights. The Light Brigade was cut off from the British lines. The shattered brigade regrouped – and charged yet again.

Once again, they managed to battle their way through the enemy but it was not over yet. Ahead lay almost a mile of open ground littered with dead and dying men and horses. Both flanks remained in the control of the Russians, and bands of Cossacks were waiting to pick off stragglers.

The first riders reached British lines just twenty minutes after Cardigan had ordered them forward. Of the 670 men who had set out, just 195 had made it back unwounded and still mounted. Sergeant Frederick Short recalled what happened next: 'On returning to the place we had originally started from I saw, for the first time since we had departed, the Earl of Cardigan, who must have arrived before us, and he came up and said, "Men, it was a hare-brained trick, but it was no fault of mine." I heard some of the men, who were naturally still rather excited, say, "Never mind my Lord, we are ready to go again."'

Watching from a nearby hill, French Marshal Pierre Bosquet is famously quoted as having said of the charge: 'C'est magnifique, mais ce n'est pas la guerre' – 'It is magnificent, but it is not war.' Less well known is the rest of his comment: 'C'est de la folie' – 'It is madness.' It was, though, a magnificent madness for reporter William Russell, whose dispatch appeared in *The Times* on 14 November:

HEIGHTS BEFORE SEBASTOPOL, OCTOBER 25[end small caps] – If the exhibition of the most brilliant valour, of the excess of courage, and of a daring which would have reflected lustre on the best days of chivalry can afford full consolation for the disaster of today, we can have no reason to regret the melancholy loss which we sustained in a contest with a savage and barbarian enemy.

It is a journalistic maxim that when faced with a choice between the truth and a story, the public will always want the story. A critic of the army's management of the war, Russell later claimed that 'our Light Brigade was annihilated by their own rashness, and by the brutality of a ferocious enemy' but for the time being, the story was not one of military incompetence but of a courage and devotion to duty that fit the buoyant mood of the nation. Just three years before, the huge glass and iron hall of the Great Exhibition had provided a showcase of Victorian power and prestige. Britain, it seemed, could achieve anything and Russell's report seemed to confirm that Britons feared nothing but failure to do their best. After reading Russell's piece, the Poet Laureate, Alfred Lord Tennyson, immediately set to work on a poem and in minutes had created a legend. Published in the *Examiner* on 9 December, his hymn of praise would set the tone for representations of the military for generations to come:

Theirs not to make reply,
Theirs not to reason why,
Theirs but to do and die:

The poem quickly became a huge success, even reaching the survivors of the charge in the Crimea itself, and thousands of copies were sold. Disastrous as the charge may have been, Tennyson's picture of the British soldier as brave, chivalrous, unquestioningly loyal and destined for glory fitted perfectly with the image of the ideal Briton. It would be these qualities that would demonstrate the moral and physical superiority of the British people as the Empire expanded.

Over the coming decades, the public were thrilled to hear stories of the heroic deeds of their army in the far-flung reaches of the world, and generations of schoolchildren learned Tennyson's poem by heart, yet the men who won those victories never found themselves accepted by the public at home. To serve in the lower ranks of the army remained an admission of failure to find a more respectable path and, for any 'decent' young man, enlistment would bring shame on his family. Although William 'Wully' Robertson had a spectacular career in which he advanced through every rank from private soldier to Field Marshal, when he first joined the 16th Lancers as a private in 1877 his horrified mother had declared, 'There are plenty of things steady young men can do when they can read and write as well as you can. I will name it to no one, I would rather bury you than see you in a red coat.' A year later, when Private Donald McDonald joined the 2nd Battalion, 21st Royal Scots Fusiliers he wrote to his brother asking him to 'let my poor mother know about it privately and not to let anyone know about it except our own family'.

In 1890 Rudyard Kipling became angry over a state of affairs he felt was hugely hypocritical. A strong supporter of the Empire, he was one of those who felt the army was suffering as a result of the negative image held by those at home. National Service, Kipling believed, would raise both the quality of the army as a whole and the status of the soldier within it. 'Tommy' was an attempt to highlight the yawning gap between the soldier as seen in wartime and the man who wore the uniform in garrison towns at home. The poem became popular, but attitudes were so entrenched that the following year an appeal to raise funds to help the veterans of the Light Brigade, now reduced to living in workhouses, raised just £24 – most of it rumoured to be the remnants of collections made by the Liberal Party to aid Irish Republican prisoners and for animal cruelty charities. Bitterly, Kipling wrote:

There were thirty million English who talked of England's might,
There were twenty broken troopers who lacked a bed for the night.
They had neither food nor money, they had neither service nor trade;
They were only shiftless soldiers, the last of the Light Brigade.

They felt that life was fleeting; they knew not that art was long,
That though they were dying of famine, they lived in deathless song.
They asked for a little money to keep the wolf from the door;
And the thirty million English sent twenty pounds and four!

O thirty million English that babble of England's might,
Behold there are twenty heroes who lack their food to-night;
Our children's children are lisping to 'honour the charge they made'
And we leave to the streets and the workhouse the charge of the
Light Brigade!

Within a decade, the Boer War had brought home to the public that the British army was equipped for small-scale tribal wars against poorly armed Indians and Africans but it could not compete with even the small but well-equipped Boers who, supported by Germany, used the latest rifles as they fought a fast-moving guerrilla war and inflicted humiliatingly heavy casualties on the British. The press and the public were furious, demanding that the army be given the proper training and equipment to fight this new enemy. Over the coming decade, reforms were brought in to improve standards.

The declaration of war against Germany in 1914 was greeted by many with enthusiasm. For years since their support for the Boers, fears of a German invasion of Britain had been growing and here was a chance to end the threat. Thanks to its pool of trained reservists who had all undergone compulsory military training for at least two years, Germany had huge numbers of men it could bring into action. Britain's small professional army was too small and ill-equipped at first to defeat the huge army Germany could field, so all its 'contemptible little army' could do was hold them off until the country could improvise another army of volunteers.

Although volunteering for the ranks was suddenly no longer a stigma and regarded as every man's duty, the eager recruits to the 'New Army' were keen to ensure that they served with the 'right' sort of person. Battalions formed around professions with very clear rules about who should be allowed to serve with whom. No one, it seemed, wanted to serve alongside men of a different social class. The city of Hull, for example, created four of the famous Pals battalions, unofficially known respectively as the 'Hull Commercials' (for shop owners and their staffs), 'Hull Tradesmen', 'Hull Sportsmen' (for members of the local football and rugby teams or other athletically minded citizens) and, for those of a lesser social standing, a battalion simply known as 'Hull t'others'.

Even the huge surge in enlistment that followed Kitchener's call in 1914 could not keep pace with demand, and after much debate, conscription was introduced in early 1916. Men of all classes were now expected to serve together and some of those who might otherwise have shunned the military took to their unexpected career change in remarkable ways.

Wilfrith Elstob was the 25-year-old son of a clergyman and was working as a school teacher when war broke out. Along with thousands of other men, he volunteered for the local Pals battalion and by 1918 commanded it with the rank of Lieutenant Colonel, having already been awarded the Distinguished Service Order and the Military Cross. In March of that year, the Germans were preparing a large offensive. The Bolshevik revolution had brought Russia's part in the war to an end and freed Germany to shift its divisions to the Western Front. A final, overwhelming attack was planned to destroy the Allies before America entered the war. In readiness, the British had prepared a zonal system of defence with a series of fortified positions intended to act like breakwaters, disrupting and disorganising any large attack so that a counterattack could be launched. Elstob and the men of his 16th Battalion were given the task of defending a redoubt known as Manchester Hill, in the St. Quentin area (named in honour of its capture by the 2nd Battalion, the Manchester Regiment in 1917).

On 18 March, Colonel Elstob gathered his men together and fully explained to them the system of defence. It was known that a full-scale attack was imminent and that they had been selected to bear the brunt of the first onslaught. The Divisional Commander had told Elstob, 'It must be impressed upon all troops allotted to the defence of any position, whether in the outpost system or the main battle position, that so far as they are concerned there is only one degree of resistance, and that is to the last round and to the last man.' Looking around, Elstob could see the faces of men he had joined up with, men whose families he knew. Pointing to a blackboard showing the battalion's positions he said, 'This is Battalion Headquarters. Here we fight and here we die.' That evening, the battalion began their march to the hill. Soon after they left camp, the band was ordered to turn back. Watching them go, Elstob commented, 'Those are the only fellows that will come out alive.'

Three days later, at 6.30am, a furious gas and artillery barrage hit Manchester Hill. For two hours it pounded the positions until, shrouded by smoke and a fog that had formed around the hill, the enemy closed in. By 2.00pm most of the defenders of Manchester Hill were either dead or wounded and vicious hand-to-hand fighting was taking place all around. At 3.30pm, Colonel Elstob spoke on the phone to a Staff Officer saying that very few were left and that the end was nearly come. But, he insisted, 'The Manchester Regiment will defend Manchester Hill to the last.' With a final 'goodbye', he hung up. The 29-year-old colonel was killed soon after when he refused to surrender, firing his pistol into a group of Germans as they forced their way into the last trench on Manchester Hill. His actions that day won an obscure former schoolteacher the Victoria Cross and considerably delayed the German offensive, buying time for a counterattack to be prepared. It was just one of a series of similar actions taking place along the Western Front as the Kaiserschlacht (the 1918 Spring Offensive) hit. All along the line, men who had never dreamed of soldiering found themselves fighting to the last to hold ground.

By the time Elstob died, soldiering had not only lost its stigma, it had become expected without question that a man should serve in uniform. Yet the end of the war saw another shift in public opinion. If the powers of the military under the Protectorate had harmed the way the public viewed the military, then the enforcement of conscription and the seeming abandonment of veterans by the government once the war was over created a massive political backlash. During the postwar years of economic downturn that made the return to civilian life difficult for the citizen soldiers who had served 'for the duration', the Allied victory was all but forgotten. All that remained was a sense of futility and waste; of a war of 'lions led by donkeys'.

This highly charged political atmosphere helped to prevent the government from introducing conscription until the outbreak of war in 1939. Defence cuts after 1918 had been drastic and as before, an army had to be improvised to reinforce one that lacked the training and equipment for the task ahead. Confounding the problem was indecision over how best to use the manpower available. Those who could avoided service for as long as possible and those who were called up found themselves allocated to any of the three services seemingly on a whim. Often, those with skills or qualifications would be siphoned off quickly to the navy and air force where the demand for skilled men seemed most obvious despite Liddell-Hart's 1935 warning that 'the unskilled man in the Services, as in industry, is losing his utility. Quality outweighs quantity on the modern battlefield.' Still, the lower the quality of recruit, the greater his chances of being allocated to the army. In October 1939 General Sir Frederick Pile, Commander-in-Chief of Anti-Aircraft Command, received an unplanned intake of 11,000 'immatures' from all divisions (soldiers returned to the UK from France because they were under 19 years of age and therefore too young to serve overseas). He reported that at a 'fairly representative battery' an intake of 25 conscripts included one man with 'a withered arm, one was mentally deficient, one had no thumbs [...] one had a glass eye which fell out whenever he doubled to the guns'. Of 1,000 recruits to 31st Anti-Aircraft Brigade, Pile estimated that as many as one in ten was either mentally or psychologically unsuitable 'even considered against an undemanding standard'.

The army set about instilling a set of rules and drills that even the most awkward soldier could manage. It was forced to work to the lowest common denominator and, as millions of ex-soldiers can testify, that ensured that the very first lesson of army life every private soldier learns is, 'you're not paid to think!' It was an attitude that ran throughout World War II and into the period of compulsory National Service that ran from 1949 to 1960. It earned the British army a reputation for being a slow, methodical, plodding organisation in which the key qualities of the frontline soldier of initiative and intelligence had been stifled. In films, plays and books that proliferated after the war, the image of the young soldier as someone unable to think for himself, waiting only for orders from his officers and following them blindly, quickly emerged. It has been too readily retained in the collective imagination.

By the end of National Service, every family in the country had a connection with the forces, and having a son, brother, husband or father in uniform lost its stigma. Half a century after the last conscript was discharged, the army has reverted to its former outsider status, its members once again viewed with suspicion.

Almost 120 years after the publication of Kipling's 'Tommy', film maker Mark Ashmore's film *Broken Britain* asked different difficult questions about the way soldiers are treated in Britain today. 'The film,' he explains, 'is about soldiers coming back [from Afghanistan] and not being able to get into a pub because there's a sign outside that reads: "No hoodies, no track suit bottoms, no soldiers". It's about what that sign represents in modern society. It's discrimination and to not let them over the threshold of a public house – what does that say about us?'

Former paratrooper Barry Phillips, who starred in the film, says that it was based on a number of real incidents. 'You do all the training and you can handle the day-to-day grime, but it's when you come home to your country after fighting for it to find out that you can't even go into a pub. It's very common especially in the big garrison towns like Colchester and Aldershot.'

In July 2007 a new 30-bed ward was added to the existing 170 beds at the Headley Court Rehabilitation Centre to cope with the growing numbers of forces personnel injured in Iraq and Afghanistan. The charity Soldiers, Sailors, Airmen and Families Association (SSAFA) sought planning permission to convert a seven-bedroom house in the nearby village of Ashtead for use by up to six families of veterans being treated at the centre. It would be adapted to be fully accessible so men and women undergoing treatment at Headley Court could visit or stay overnight with their families.

Citing increased traffic, loss of privacy for neighbours, fears that residents would not feel part of the community or that burglars could easily pretend to be visitors, over eighty objections were made. Residents complained that the scheme would cause 'harm to a quiet residential area'. After 'overwhelming' local opposition, the local council admitted it was an 'emotive issue, but that based purely its planning merits', the application should be refused because it would 'adversely impact the quiet, peaceful nature of the existing area'. 'Do people think,' asked Sue Norton, whose husband Peter was awarded the George Cross for bravery after losing a leg and part of an arm in Iraq, 'that families visiting injured servicemen are going to be out partying?' Her two young sons had barely been able to see their father because of the long round trip from their home, and their relationship with him as he readjusted was suffering as a result. 'This sort of facility,' she told reporters, 'is something that should have been in place a long time ago – they have them in America and Germany, but in the British system we have to make do.'

Elsewhere, antipathy to the army was common. At a parents' evening at a London school, one mother stood up to express alarm that her son had told her he was considering joining up. 'Had the school encouraged this in some subversive way and had any other parents had similar experiences?' wrote Sarah Sands, herself the mother of a serving soldier. 'Imagine substituting the word "doctor" or "lawyer" for armed forces and you see how far removed we have become from "our boys". We may glimpse soldiers rumbling past in Land Rovers or avoid them on late-night trains to Aldershot. We sentimentalise them for risking their lives but are squeamish about battle victories. We use them as ballast for our dinner party conversations about the war in Iraq but do not imagine them as husbands, or sons or brothers.' Nor indeed as wives, mothers, daughters and sisters.

Glorified and vilified, saint and sinner, everyone has an opinion about soldiers, but behind the headlines and heroism, who are they?

CHAPTER TWO
THE 'TOMMY'

When archaeologist David Thorpe found himself tracked down in the middle of the Jordanian desert by a group of British soldiers who had been following his team's research into the exploits of T.E. Lawrence and the Great Arab Revolt via an internet blog, he was, to say the least, surprised by their interest. He was even more surprised when, as a result of the meeting, he was invited by the Headquarters of British Forces Cyprus to accompany their annual Battlefield Tour expedition. 'David, the left-wing [archaeologist] and a bunch of hard-core soldiers? Not a match made in heaven you'd think,' he later said. 'But you'd be wrong. I spent nine days with twenty-five members of BFC, both male and female.' Almost all had served in Afghanistan or Iraq or both. Most were due back there soon afterwards. 'I learnt an inestimable amount from the serving soldiers. They have a view of the terrain, its difficulties and obstructions, military practicalities, and varying insights that I hope to bring to our [study]. I can honestly say it was a pleasure to learn from a Lance Corporal and a cavalry officer, to mention only two. On a personal note, I came back to the UK with an entirely different point of view of British service personnel. This is going to sound trite, but they were insightful, highly disciplined, respectful of our Jordanian hosts, willing to learn, and extremely tolerant of this rather radical archaeologist. And, yes, bloody intelligent. How naïve I must have been – thank you tabloid press. Damn good laugh, too!' The experience had been, he said 'one of the most enlightening and enjoyable weeks of my life'.

Aboard the *Canberra*, sailing with the Falklands Task Force in 1982, *Observer* journalist Patrick Bishop found that the troops 'spoke with the accents of Britain's unemployment black-spots' but were 'fanatically clean and tidy [...] They were friendly and cheerful too and courteous to a degree that was so at odds with the norm in the civilian world that we [journalists] were always suspicious that our legs were being pulled.' Almost thirty years later, journalist Dylan Jones also found the courtesy surprising among soldiers in Afghanistan: 'There is an orthodoxy and a sense of order about Camp Bastion that you don't expect. Not on a military base in the middle of a war zone, not in this part of Helmand, anyway. Efficiency is implicit, and among the rush and the push there is a feeling of genuine calm. Here in Helmand, rigour is de rigueur, and you immediately feel that everyone around you knows exactly what they're meant to be doing at every minute of the day. Politeness prevails, too. When lives are at stake, where's the sense in petty squabbles? For the visitor, the atmosphere is strangely seductive, as you begin to think this is what society actually ought to be like, a community of dedicated, courteous people who are too busy worrying about the macro to busy themselves with the micro.'

It's a theme that recurs whenever a liberal, well-educated professional encounters the army for the first time – a sense of surprise that the people they meet are not the blindly obedient, unimaginative, dim-witted but loyal cannon fodder they had expected, but intelligent, motivated individuals who see their job as worthwhile and who take pride in doing it well. They are, in short, professionals and respectable in every sense of the word. But then 'respectable' has never been a word society has associated with the soldier.

So who are they?

THE TOMS

No one knows for certain where the name originated. A letter about a mutiny in Jamaica in 1743 noted 'except for those from N. America (mostly Irish Papists) ye Marines and Tommy Atkins behaved splendidly'. By 1815, the name had been adopted by the War Office and used to illustrate how the various forms should be completed. The name stuck. Over the years, Tommy Atkins became simply Tommy and today the ordinary British soldier is simply known to his friends as Tom.

As a career choice goes, there are easier ways to make a living. In 2010 the average salary of a newly qualified soldier is around £17,000 before tax. For this, once in the combat zone he or she is likely to be on duty for at least sixteen hours every day which means an hourly rate of about £2.95 (the national minimum wage for those aged 18–21 is £4.83). As one pupil at a selective grammar school explained to Julia Stuart of the *Independent*, the army was not a choice for him. He wanted to be a lawyer instead because of 'the whole danger aspect and how you could actually die. I think my mum would be quite worried if I wanted to join. At a guess, I think a soldier would earn about £20,000. A barrister would earn probably more, and salary would matter to me. One of my ambitions is to be quite wealthy and have nice things.' Another told her: 'It would be hard work and I'm not really interested. You wake up early, then there's all the activities like running. You have to carry everything on your back all the time. I would rather get a degree and then get a job. I wouldn't want to risk my life either. You have to join at 17 or 18. I'd rather have a social life with my friends.' A third explained: 'The army doesn't appeal. Life as a soldier would probably be very challenging and rewarding. But there are some feelings of contempt against the army around. The hours might not be good and going away for months at a time can't be easy. I suppose soldiers do a good job. It's just not always seen to be that way.'

Colonel Jonathan Calder-Smith of the army's recruitment office explains how he sees 'gatekeepers – teachers and parents, mothers particularly – who are less keen to see their sons and daughters joining the army and that is understandable, but there are more people who come in and say something along the lines of 'I want to do my bit' – people who have seen what is happening and want to step up to the plate.'

People like Blake Franklin, another pupil at the school. 'I want to make a difference,' he said. 'The money doesn't attract me, it's the lifestyle: getting to travel a lot and the opportunity to learn more languages and skills and meet more people. I would be happy to die for my country. It's something I've discussed with my parents. I've got a passion for the country and want to be the best at what I do, and to be the best you have to take risks and that's one of them [...] I feel proud of the army, particularly when they capture people like Saddam Hussein. However, when you see hooligans beat people up it doesn't make me feel proud. But they're a small minority. I'm patriotic because my country has given me a lot.'

The simple soldier is a complex beast and the reasons given for joining up are many and varied. One, however, is always to the fore. It's often been said that unemployment is the best recruiting sergeant. Today, sociologists and politicians speak instead of 'economic conscription' but it amounts to the same thing, assuming soldiers join because they have nowhere else to go, perpetuating the myth that the army is a refuge for the unemployed and unemployable. The huge surge of volunteers enlisting at the outbreak of the World War I has been partly attributed to a slump in the economy, which meant men were happy to join up for a war promised to be over by Christmas in return for food, uniform and lodgings.

Keeping the modern army up to strength in a time of relatively low unemployment has been difficult. Concerns were raised in 2005 about the number of Commonwealth citizens being recruited to fill the gaps – so great was the influx that in one regiment as many as one in five soldiers was recruited from outside the UK. As Alan Whitelaw, the Regimental Colonel of the Royal Regiment of Scotland, told the *Daily Telegraph* in 2008: 'Over the past two years, recruitment has been markedly down, which is a factor of a strong economy. It is true that when there is an economic downturn, recruitment tends to go up.' In the hardest hit areas, recruitment goes up, while in areas less affected by the downturn, local regiments remain under strength.

It's a situation about which many opponents of the military are angry. When the army opened three recruitment 'showrooms' in London and Kent where potential recruits could meet serving soldiers, fierce criticism was received: 'It seems that the government's response to recruitment problems is to target younger and younger people from more and more disadvantaged areas,' said Angus Mulready-Jones, a Labour councillor in one of the areas selected. 'That is the only reasonable explanation for opening this showroom in Hackney [...] It seems to me that we are limiting the aspirations of people in areas like this. We have a huge shortage of social workers, planners and NHS staff but instead of offering training for worthwhile long-term employment, we are spending hundreds of thousands of pounds on these fancy recruitment centres that give a very one-sided view of life in the army.'

Opponents of the army's targeted recruitment on disadvantaged areas have reason to be concerned. Project 100,000 was an attempt launched in 1966 by the US military to offer military training and discipline to disadvantaged youths in order to 'rehabilitate' those termed 'the subterranean poor'. Young men with little or no education, some with an IQ in the low 60s, were enlisted into the US military where their poor aptitude scores meant that they were found fit only for frontline infantry duty in the so-called 'US Moron Corps' and shipped to Vietnam, where their casualty rate was found to be almost double that of the men who enlisted normally. With a high proportion of black and ethnic minority youths involved, Project 100,000 soon came to be seen by critics as a cynical ploy to reduce the ranks of the underclass.

The showrooms, though, are not part of a Project 100,000-style social experiment. The recession may have had a big impact on the numbers coming forward but, as Colonel Calder-Smith explained, from the army's point of view, 'We are happy to see an increase in candidates as long as they have the ability and skills to make it through the training and succeed in the army.' An increase in the numbers coming forward, after all, means the army is in a position to select better candidates from a wider pool.

Like their ancestors of 1914, though, joblessness may be a factor in a decision to enlist, but it is only one factor and frequently a minor one. In 1982 the BBC followed a group of recruits to the Parachute Regiment and found that, 'Although the recession was at its height, very few of them had been noticeably affected by unemployment. Certainly some had – four of them from Scotland and the North had been unemployed for a year or more – but this was exceptional, and in only two cases could it really be considered a serious factor in their joining the army. Half the intake had been involved in some kind of apprenticeship or training scheme, and a fair number had completed their time as tradesmen. So the decision to join the army seemed to have little to do with personal inadequacies or a hostile environment.' As Brigadier Jolyon Jackson, the head of army recruitment, said at the time, 'People take the decision to join the army very seriously – you can't walk into a recruitment office one day and get in the next day. It is a long and strenuous process.'

At the Army Careers office, the potential recruit will sit a computer-based touch-screen psychometric test known as the British Army Recruit Battery (BARB). This, alongside a literacy and numeracy test, is designed to assess the candidate's ability to assimilate the training required for their chosen trade. They will also attend a number of interviews to decide on overall suitability for the army. The recruiting staff will also check references from schools or any employers, proof of identification, nationality and residency, and conduct a preliminary medical questionnaire, which is completed by the candidate and their family GP.

If these initial tests and interviews are passed successfully, the potential recruit is booked for further tests at one of the Recruit Selection Centres (Lichfield or Pirbright in England, Glencorse in Scotland or Ballymena in Northern Ireland). The recruit then goes to the centre for two days during which they undergo a thorough medical examination, physical assessment tests which include pull ups, static dynamic weight lift, back extension test, 150 metre jerry can carry and a 2.4 km (1.5 mile) best-effort run. There are also some team games held in the evening. They also sit a Technical Selection Test, a paper exam for those applying for specialist trades. There are further interviews, team-building exercises, practice lessons and a chance to speak to recruits in training. Only at the end of this is the candidate offered a place to start training. It's a demanding process and it's meant to be. Only those who are determined to join complete the process. Then comes a wait of up to several months before a vacancy on a training course comes up.

TAMMY ATKINS

For Private Michelle Norris, a career in the army had been a long-held dream. 'I remember sitting on my dad's knee watching old war movies and documentaries, because he loves his history. I remember watching *The Battle of Britain* and we could both say the words before they came out of the actors' mouths. And the next morning, I would wake up thinking, 'I want to be a soldier. I want to do all that.' After completing school, with hopes of joining the Royal Artillery, 'I went up for selection as soon as I could, but I failed on my fitness: I took two seconds too long on the mile-and-a-half run and I could only do two pull-ups and you had to do four.'

Disheartened by her failure, Norris spent a year at college before trying again. This time she cut a full two minutes off her running time and managed nine pull-ups but by now her plans had changed. She joined the RAMC and after nine months' training was posted to Germany with 1 Close Support Medical Regiment. 'After a while, they said they were looking for volunteers for Iraq and I thought that was what I wanted to join for, so I just put my hand straight up.' Norris went on to become the first woman to win the Military Cross for bravery under fire in 2007.

Receiving the award, she told reporters, 'I know some people doubt whether we can work properly on the front line. A lot of people say women can't do this, women can't go on the front line, I hope I've proved we can.'

From the campaign of Joan of Arc to today, military history is filled with stories of women in uniform: Hannah Snell served in Guise's Regiment of Foot in 1745 before moving on to the navy where she was involved in hand-to-hand fighting in India and wounded several times before retiring from the navy with a pension and opening the Female Warrior pub in Wapping. When Phoebe Hessel died in Brighton in 1821 aged 107, the King himself paid for her funeral as a mark of respect for a woman who, rather than be left behind when her husband joined the army, followed him and served for 17 years as a soldier in the 5th Regiment of Foot. At least 50 women fought in the American Civil War and, in World War I, a 25-year-old Russian peasant girl named Maria Botchkareva managed (with the support of an amused local commander) to get permission from the Czar to enlist as a regular soldier. Despite her initial problems of fighting off the frequent sexual advances and ridicule of her male comrades, she fought alongside them in battle – including an incident in which she bayoneted a German soldier to death. When the anti-Bolshevik forces seemed to be wavering after the 1917 Revolution, Botchkareva proposed setting up the Battalion of Death, a force of 2,000 women whose role 'would be to shame the men in the trenches by having the women go over the top first'. Although little more than a propaganda tool, the battalion did lead one attack and proved, as Botchkareva later put it, 'they were no longer women, but soldiers'.

Despite such examples, and the even greater use by the Russians of female regiments during the World War II, attitudes in the West were very different. It was widely regarded that women could not physically or emotionally face the rigours of combat and so great was the assumption that women could not serve in combat zones that nurses for the US Military working at MASH hospitals in Korea later found that while their male colleagues were entitled to veterans' benefits for their service, they were not.

British Special Operations Executive agents proved that women could be highly effective in mounting insurgency operations, but the regular military remained of the opinion that women had no role in combat operations. When women of the Ulster Defence Regiment were deployed in Northern Ireland to assist in searches, senior officers insisted that they dress in skirts to clearly identify them as women and therefore deter snipers shooting them. As Ulster veteran Ken Wharton explains, 'the terrorists used "shoot and scoot" tactics firing into the backs of Land Rovers as they were going away from them. All they had to do was shoot between the tail lights and they would hit something, skirts or trousers, it did not matter.'

All military trades have their own radio callsign. Starlight was used to indicate the medical staff, Sheldrake the artillery. Callsigns for women soldiers were a product of their time: Manhole for admin staff, Coffeepot for female Military Police, Rucbag for women of the Royal Ulster Constabulary. The decision was taken in 1990, as women deployed to the first Gulf War, that it was no longer necessary to have a separate Women's Royal Army Corps. As of 1991, they would join Corps and regiments in the same way as men and work alongside them except for those units whose primary task is 'to close with and kill the enemy face-to-face'.

Captain Kirstie Main of the Royal Artillery explains the role of women in the modern military:

I'm often asked what it's like being a woman in a male-dominated environment. But I am no different – I have done the same training, the same fitness tests, the same exercises as every guy. There really is no difference between male and female. Women still do not fight on the front line. But as we are no longer fighting conventional warfare, there is no clearly defined front line. When the enemy is everywhere, the front line is everywhere. In Afghanistan, women regularly did the same job as men in the same areas. It is more common than most people think. Since the first Gulf War, or Bosnia, the role of women has changed because the nature of warfare has changed and the rule that women should not fight on the front line has become obsolete and should be scrapped. You're in the army to be part of the action. That's what I want and I think it is unfair that my opportunities are limited [...] I want the public to know what women in the forces do. Every day they do work that puts them at risk. Where I was based in Afghanistan, we had soldiers injured and killed, and they could have been women. There were women in vehicles behind them, in the troops near them. The public may not think that women are on the front line, but they are. If you asked the lads who fought alongside me, they would say that I was just one of the lads as well.

RUPERTS

The only reason a soldier would follow this officer is out of idle curiosity.

Lt Colonel Benton

In the wake of the English Civil war and the harsh regime of Cromwell's Protectorate, fear of a professional army like that raised by Parliament against the King threatened the status quo, so command of the remodelled army went to men who could afford to purchase a commission and who had a vested interest in maintaining their status and wealth – men who had nothing to gain by overthrowing the monarchy. Skill and ability were welcome attributes but never seen as an essential requirement for the job of commanding troops. At the start of the Napoleonic Wars the Adjutant-General complained that of the 26 regiments available to him, 21 were 'commanded literally by boys or idiots'. With neither the will nor the financial investment needed to improve the quality of the army by requiring its officers to undergo training, it gradually became the dumping ground for otherwise unemployable young gentlemen. When the purchase of commissions was abolished in 1871, restrictions were put in place instead to ensure that 'the right sort' held sway. In many regiments, private income was mandatory and military historian Richard Holmes has noted that in 1903, the War Office estimated that an infantry officer needed a private income of £160 per year over and above his army pay just to keep afloat at a time when a large family home in London could be rented for about £100 per year. A middle-class professional might manage to earn an annual salary in the region of £500, but an officer in one of the 'better' cavalry units would expect to need to have an average £600–700 (more than enough to buy a house in the Home Counties) every year to cover his mess bills, horses and uniform. It is said that in one of the fashionable cavalry regiments, a newly arrived subaltern was told that the War Office had credited his account with £100. 'Good God,' he replied, 'do they actually pay us?'

If the life of an officer in peacetime seemed no different from joining a very agreeable club, membership had its price. In the many wars in which the Victorian army found itself embroiled, their role became a simple one. According to Desmond Morton, 'they gave leadership, took responsibility, and set an example, if necessary, by dying [...] Implicit was the assumption that the officer would be the first to die in battle.' Whatever their social differences, on active service an officer had a very clear duty to his men. Asked where his officers were, one NCO replied simply: 'When it comes time to die, they'll be with us.' In return, officers gained the respect of the men they led and, among many regimental officers, a strong mutual bond of loyalty grew from the shared dangers they faced. It was a curiously patronising relationship where teenage boys held the power of life and death over men old enough to be their fathers yet felt the need to look after their men as though they were children. 'The more helpless a position in which an officer finds his men,' wrote Sir Garnet Wolseley in the wake of the Zulu War of 1879, 'the more it is his bounden duty to stay and share their fortune, whether for good or ill. It is because the British officer has always done so that he possesses the influence he does in the ranks of our army. The soldier has learned to feel that come what may, he can in the direst moment of danger look with implicit faith to his officer, knowing that he will never desert him under any possible circumstances.'

That view was shared by the Reverend Studdart-Kennedy, who won the Military Cross in World War I: 'Live with the men, go everywhere they go. Make up your mind you will take their risks, and more, if you can do any good. The line is the key to the whole business. Work in the very front and they will listen to you; but if you stay behind you are wasting your time. Men will forgive you anything but lack of courage and devotion.' The relationship between an officer and his men was, and is, a relationship best summed up in the legend that tells of a young officer urging his men forward into an attack until his sergeant took him to one side and explained quietly that 'the correct form of words, sir, is "follow me"'.

To the men who serve under them, officers are always Ruperts (pronounced 'Wooperts') and hold one of four main types of commission:

The Short Service Commission
The SSC is the normal first commission for between 3 and 8 years for those who become an officer in the army but don't want to commit to a long career in the army.

The Intermediate Regular Commission
This lasts for a maximum of 18 years. On completion of 18 years after the age of 40, the officer will be entitled to a lump sum and regular monthly payments, which will convert at 65 to a further lump sum and pension.

The Regular Commission
This offers a full career of 35 years or to age 60, whichever comes first. Those completing a full career will receive an immediate lump sum and pension from age 55.

Late Entry Commissions

A number of senior Non Commissioned Officers and Warrant Officers can be granted commissions known as Late Entry Commissions. They attend the Late Officer Entry Course at Sandhurst but because of their age they generally do not rise above the rank of Lieutenant Colonel. To the men, LEC officers are usually known more or less affectionately as 'Rodneys'.

The old stereotype lives on. The 'chinless wonder' fresh out of Sandhurst still fills the hearts of experienced NCOs with dread, but they are getting fewer. Aboard the *Canberra* en route to the Falklands, Patrick Bishop noted that, like their men, the officers he met 'came as a surprise. I had vaguely imagined a group of gently bred, ill-educated reactionaries. It was true that some of them spoke in that contorted way that made the order "fan out" sound like "fair night", that the troops could mimic so well, but among the Marine officers in particular there were many who spoke in the same accents as their men.'

'Heartbreakingly young' is how Dylan Jones described the young soldiers he encountered in Afghanistan. In 2009, within days of his eighteenth birthday, Fusilier Hayden Hendricks of 2nd Battalion, the Royal Regiment of Fusiliers left for Afghanistan and became the youngest of the 8,300 British troops in that theatre of operations. Even having spent seven months in pre-deployment training, he is not unusual. A recruit can enlist at 16 years of age for soldiers or 17 for officers, and as many as 40 per cent of British troops join the army at an age when they are legally still regarded as children.

The legends surrounding the boy soldiers of the Great War have tended to romanticise the experiences of a relative few. Certainly many thousands of underage recruits attempted to enlist in the tidal wave of patriotism that marked the outbreak of war in 1914, but only those who could maintain the pretence made it to the trenches. John Condon was reputedly the youngest British casualty when he was killed in 1915 and his Commonwealth War Graves headstone gives his age as just 14.

Research, however, has shown that this was a transcription error. Condon's service record shows he joined the army in 1913, a year before the war. That he added a year to his age is true, but to persuade even the keenest recruiting sergeant in peacetime that a 12-year-old boy was really 18 seems unlikely. In fact, any soldier under the age of 19 was classified as 'immature' under military law and could not be sent overseas. Even at its lowest ebb, the British army's minimum age for service in France was 18 years and 6 months, provided the soldier had had at least six months' training in the UK. In 1940 the British Expeditionary Force lost the equivalent of an entire division because they were deemed too young to go to war.

It was only later, in the second half of the twentieth century, that Britain deliberately sent children to war. In 1982 Mark Eyles-Thomas travelled to the Falklands with three friends – Jason Burt, Ian 'Scrivs' Scrivens and Neil Grose. They had met in the Junior Parachute Company which was responsible for training 16-year-old school-leavers and the group were posted to the 3rd Battalion. On the night of 11–12 June, the four of them were preparing to go into battle for the heavily defended summit of Mount Longdon, overlooking the Falklands capital of Port Stanley. As they moved forward in the darkness, their section commander, Corporal Brian Milne, stepped on an anti-personnel mine and suddenly the element of surprise was gone.

In his book *Sod That For a Game of Soldiers,* Mark takes up the story:

'Mount Longdon, previously cold, dark and still, had now come alive. The mountain and our initial objective were still 100 yards away to my right. Our section, now out in the open land of the minefield, was vulnerable to the enemy's gunfire. Cpl Milne's screams reduced to the horrendous groans of a man in serious pain.'

The section was ordered to take out an Argentine position, but as they moved into the attack, both Jason Burt and Neil Grose were hit by small arms fire.

'Jas?' I called out. Nothing came back. 'Tom, is that you?' a voice asked. Tom was my nickname. 'Is that you, Scrivs?' I said. 'Yeah, I'm over here with Grose. He's been shot.'

I crawled back to look for Jas and spotted him lying face-down about 30ft from where I had taken cover. I called to him, but he didn't answer. A round from a machine gun had penetrated his head, killing him instantly.

Then I crawled over to Scrivs, who was with Grose in the middle of the battlefield. 'I think he's been shot in the chest,' said Scrivs. 'But I can't find the exit wound.' Each time a shot rang out, Scrivs would lie over Grose, whose birthday it was, to protect him. 'How're you enjoying your birthday party, mate?' Scrivs jokingly quizzed Grose. 'You certainly know how to have a do. I think the neighbours will be upset with the noise, though.' Grose tried to laugh, but the pain was too much. 'Don't make me laugh,' he pleaded. 'We're going to have to move him,' I said to Scrivs. I placed my hand on Scrivs' shoulder to beckon his head nearer to mine. At that very moment a single shot rang out.

Scrivs fell across my lap and fluid splattered on my face. I pushed Scrivs off me with an instinctive and repulsive jerk. He lay motionless in a limp, crumpled heap. I sat there not believing what had happened. One minute I was talking to Scrivs with my hand on his shoulder, the next – ZAP – he was gone.

Then Grose looked at me. 'Where's Scrivs?' he asked. I didn't want to tell him, but he could see it in my eyes. Grose screwed up his eyes, this time in the pain of losing a friend, and tears fell. I cried, too.

Mark carried Grose back to safety but his injuries were too severe. Neil Grose, oldest of the four young Paras, died on his eighteenth birthday.

In 2007 the BBC revealed that between 2003 and 2005, fifteen 17-year-old British soldiers, four of them female, were inadvertently sent to Iraq despite Britain having, on 24 June 2003, ratified the UN Optional

Protocol to the Convention on the Rights of the Child on the involvement of children in armed conflict to ensure that under-18s were not deployed to war zones. Defence Minister Adam Ingram admitted that although the UK would not condone the deployment of anyone under the age of eighteen, 'Unfortunately, these processes are not infallible and the pressures on units prior to deployment have meant that there have been a small number of instances where soldiers have been inadvertently deployed to Iraq before their eighteenth birthday.' They may be children when they leave, but after accompanying a patrol of the 2nd Rifles in Afghanistan in August 2009, journalist Michael Yon concluded: 'Some of the soldiers out here might seem young, but there are no young soldiers here. Not even one.'

BASIC TRAINING

There was never anything in the tea. Generations of young men have believed that 'they' put something in it – bromide was always the favourite culprit – to stop young men having the sort of thoughts young men always have. Instead, for the new recruit away from home for probably the first time, the loss of libido had nothing to do with drugs, just culture shock.

'The change from civilian to soldier is not one that is easily accomplished,' wrote Leslie Vickers in 1917:

We soon find that there are many new conditions to be faced, many new and uncongenial tasks to be undertaken, and all sorts of strange and novel regulations to which we must render strictest obedience [...] In military life things are all changed. We become at once cogs in the great machine. We have a definite work to perform. The smooth running of the plant depends on us. We lose much of our independence. We realise that other cogs depend on us and, further, that there are many bigger cogs who drive us and whose bigness and authority we must thoroughly appreciate and recognise [...] There may be occasions when we thoroughly despise our seniors and conclude that everything military was arranged for our oppression. Bit by bit we shall lose the conviction that we 'know it all' already, and as knowledge increases within us, we shall appreciate more and more the knowledge and experience of those placed over us. Regulations and even red tape will be seen to have a wise purpose, though, to the end of our days, we may long for some official scissors to cut it.

The change from civilian to soldier is produced in one way only – THE LEARNING OF OBEDIENCE. This is the first and last lesson. The civilian is only obedient in certain ways and to a limited extent. The soldier is obedient in every way and to any extent, even to death [...] It is the heart of the system. Obedience is given to some one by every rank in the army, from the highest general to the humblest private.

When we have learned obedience we need to learn discipline – for the two words do not mean exactly the same thing. Discipline may be of two kinds. First of all there is SELF-DISCIPLINE. This includes the restraint of selfishness; the cultivation of the spirit of comradeship, generosity and thoughtfulness. Then there is ARMY DISCIPLINE, which includes obedience, thoroughness, common sense and resourcefulness.

'Basic training,' says the army's website, 'is a progressive package where we take you as the raw material and develop your potential through a series of phases which increasingly demand higher standards as you become better able to match them. We will always be asking you to give your best effort and we will unlock reserves of stamina and endurance you did not realise you possessed. Our philosophy is to train you into the Army not to select you out.'

The British Army's ethos is, as it always has been, very different from other European armies. The idea of the conscript as a 'citizen in uniform' and a regime where long hair and other obvious signs of individualism are freely allowed is commonplace in Europe. 'There are very few armies that still train to fight a war,' says Major Charles Hayman, editor of *Jane's World Armies*. 'The training regime here is very, very different from what it is in the rest of Europe [...] It has to be tough because wars are nasty and brutal. That sort of training is completely at odds with the sort of society we actually live in. Basic training is far more involved and tough than it was. You are going to get very, very fit – generally the fitness standard of a minor athlete. You are taking people who may be something of a couch potato and making them very fit – it is tough. A lot of people – 25 per cent – are not going to make it.'

Training breaks down into four broad phases. The first six weeks are very much an introduction to the Infantry. Phase 1 covers a multitude of subjects such as values and standards, physical training, skill at arms lessons, drill and fieldcraft. Recruits will remain in barracks and will have a lot to learn. However, parents' day on week four is a chance for them to show off and have a night off. The phase ends with the recruits receiving their berets, cap badge and a long weekend.

The second phase from weeks seven to twelve sees the final introductory exercise, the conclusion of all fieldcraft tuition and the introduction to section attacks. There is an emphasis on shooting which culminates in the shooting test. Recruits also go away for a week of adventure training.

During the third phase in weeks 13 to 19, the training focuses on teaching the recruits infantry skills. This is based around three tactical exercises, an urban skills day and a week-long camp in Altcar, near Liverpool. At the end of this period, recruits receive a regimental tie as a mark of achievement for completing all the tactical exercises.

The fourth and final phase focuses on confirmation of training received. This comes in the form of final exercise and live firing battle camp. There is also a battlefield tour to Belgium and, of course, the passing out parade.

Sociologist John Hockey studied the experiences of a group of recruits in the 1980s and argues that alongside the obvious military syllabus is another, informal but crucial form of education. For Richard A. Gabriel and Paul L. Savage, in their study of the military command structure, 'The British Army for centuries has been recognized as a highly successful socializing institution for recruits drawn from a wide array of social, racial, and ethnic backgrounds. In the British case, this phenomenon appears related to the sense of belonging to the "regiment". Equally impressive is the proven capacity of British military units to resist and not break down under unusual pressures, which in turn reinforces regimental identity and group cohesion.'

Military training is only partly about the learning of new skills. The biggest change is from people who sees themselves as civilians to those who are, first and foremost, soldiers. It is, says Hockey, a two-part process: the first is one of Civilian Role Dispossession, followed by one of Adaptation and Adjustment.

CIVILIAN ROLE DISPOSSESSION

'The first casualty of war,' says one veteran of the training process, 'is your hairstyle.' On arrival, recruits suddenly find themselves in what sociologist Erving Goffman called 'a total institution'. Every choice, every decision will be made for them. All sense of individualism is stripped away – starting with the hair. They dress alike, in baggy coveralls or ill-fitting uniform which marks them out from the smarter recruits in more senior intakes and especially from the immaculately turned out instructors. Privacy is a thing of the past. Home comforts are gone. For 16-year-olds, it's a shock to the system. 'If you're looking for sympathy, sonny,' one former Junior Soldier recalled being told, 'it's in the Oxford English Dictionary, between shit and syphilis. Now turn to the right and f*ck off sharpish like!'

It's a period of 'beastings' – change parades in which the recruits have to parade in one type of uniform and then are given perhaps two minutes to be back on parade in a completely different type of dress, changing from combat clothing to PT kit to fatigues and back; of endless drill and cleaning. It is this element of 'Bull' that stays in the memory longest.

'Bull was terrible,' says former Corporal John Inglis of his own National Service experience. 'Whilst I was in the services we had a Bull Night once a week and everything had to be spotless. If when the Old Man came around the next day all was not right, you had another Bull Night and another inspection the following day. At one camp I was at, the coal bucket had to be emptied and bulled up with steel wool. The shafts of the billet's sweeping brushes were scraped every bull night with a razor blade. On kit inspections our PT shoes were under the bed and we put varnish on them to make them sparkle. I wore belt and gaiters for two years and every night you had to blanco them and do your brasses.'

There is a story about an American family in London. They are visiting the sights and stood next to a Guardsman on sentry. The boy asked why the soldier's boots were so shiny. 'They're made of patent leather.' The two fled in terror as the furious Guardsman growled, 'They are made of SPIT AND POLISH!' As a former Guardsman explains, the process of polishing his boots to a mirrored shine is not a simple one:

Go out for a small run in your boots (if they are new) to find where the boots are going to crease. [Then,] if the boots are Parade boots (hob-nailed 'ammunition' boots), take them to a shoe/boot repair shop and get the boots 'double tapped' (extra layer of leather put on sole and heel). If they are not Parade boots don't worry about this stage. [Next] remove the laces from the boot and force damp/wet newspaper into the boot, ensuring that the whole of the toe cap is filled, and then fill up the remainder of the boot up to ankle level. It is VERY important that you force the paper in, until the boot goes hard. Replace the laces, and tie them up tightly (We were always told that the leather containing the lace holes should meet in the middle.)

Now shape the boots by pressing in any bulges that shouldn't be there, and try to push the toe caps of ammo boots upward slightly (banana shape). This prevents the boots cracking as you march, as they 'rock' (literally).

This, though, was only the first stage. As another former soldier continues, the actual process of 'bulling' boots can now begin:

1. Cover entire surface of new boots with Kiwi Parade Gloss (and to all the old sweats, mine have NEVER gone blue when it rains!).

2. Heat the smooth rounded end of a spoon to red hot and use it to 'iron' down any stipples and lumps. Move quickly and ensure there's plenty of polish between the spoon and the leather or you'll ruin the boots. This action also pushes the polish into the leather to keep them watertight. Get it just right and you'll have black socks for ever!

3. Apply a generous coat of polish with a 'putting-on' brush and keep brushing until you get a dull shine.

4. Use your 'taking off' brush (the softer one) until you get a civvy shine.

5. Wrap a yellow duster around a finger (just one thickness of duster) and dip it into warm polish (a new tin – not the one you used for brushing). Make circular motions in the polish until it has warmed up further and soaked into the duster. You will end up with a black finger, but that's part of the game.

6. Transfer the polish onto one boot using circular motions until the entire boot is covered.

7. Do the same with the other boot. From here on, whatever you do to one boot, you do to the other to the same degree before going on to the next instruction or repeating an action. If you don't, you'll end up with odd boots!

8. Spit on a small area of the polished boot and, without moving

your finger from its position in the duster, polish the boot with wide circular motions. The spit reacts with the polish to bond the layers together. Keep spitting on different parts of the boot until all areas have been covered. Work quickly during the spit phase.

9.   Repeat from 6 to 8 many times until a lustre starts to develop.

10. Now move your finger to a different part of the duster, pick up a small amount of polish and work it over as large an area as possible, the aim being to apply a very thin coat. Keep doing this until the whole boot is covered.

11. Using very cold water, buff the polish using light circular movements. Keep buffing until the polish starts to shine. On a hot day, do this bit with the boot in a fridge or freezer or you'll be there all day. Otherwise do it under cold running water, but then you'll have a sink to clean and polish isn't easy to remove from porcelain!

12. Repeat 10 and 11 until you're quite impressed with the shine that develops.

13. Repeat 10 but with a linen handkerchief, making sure that there are no creases in the cloth under your finger.

14. Repeat 11 but with a linen handkerchief and NO water. Be very gentle.

15. Get the wife's best newest tights, or the girlfriend's stockings or your best mate's wife's tights and twist them into a tight ball, finishing with a smooth layer, no wrinkles. Very, very gently, use circular movements to finish the boots to a high gloss.

16. Try to get polish off finger. Vim, Swarfega and Fairy Liquid help but there's no substitute for a new white towel.

It seems like a lot of effort (and it is) but you can trog across the moors, soak them, scrape them to buggery and once they're dry, they will polish back up within a few minutes. (Okay – it may take up to half an hour.)

Unsurprisingly, despite their best efforts, some soldiers never quite come up to scratch. The same soldier went on:

Having joined the TA just after Recruit Camp, I had nearly a year to wait to go through the two weeks' training (at that time there was only one course each year). That gave me plenty of time to get a deep shine on my boots, experimenting with different methods to achieve the best results. The Recruit Camp allocated one hour each evening solely to boot cleaning – brush polishing the working boots and bulling the best boots. As my second pair only needed the dust blowing off them, this gave me extra time to do other things. Come the first Friday, we were informed that if the whole billet had satisfactory best boots, we'd be given the Saturday afternoon off – boots to be inspected at 22:00 that evening. One lad had been hopeless at bulling. We rallied round and tried to get a reasonable shine on his boots – only to find that when we weren't looking, he'd taken a brush to them! D'oh! Unsurprisingly, at 22:00, when the corporal inspected our boots, he wasn't satisfied. But he wanted Saturday afternoon off as well, so he gave the bloke a second-chance show at midnight.

We tried, but at 23:45 the boots still hadn't achieved a decent shine, so I gave him my boots to show. Apparently the corporal was very impressed. So impressed, in fact, that he gouged the polish out of the toe of one boot with the comment 'Perhaps now your mate won't be so keen on lending his boots to you.' We got the time off, though, so it was a small price to pay. Gouges look nasty but they're easy enough to repair.

Bernard McCabe remembered a similar parade in his own training days when his platoon Sergeant 'threw my boots out the window because they didn't meet his exacting standards. Pity the window was shut as it ruined my boots as they made their way through, and to cap it he made me pay for the window because I should have known he was going to throw them out! Oh happy days.'

Kenneth Kingsley, who joined the army in 1943, found that instructors could always find something to fault:

One particular day on parade, our little bald-headed Sergeant Major walked down our lines and inspected us to see we were smart and well-shaven. Well, aged 18, my chin was smooth as a baby's bottom. However, when he stopped in front of me he took two smart paces towards me. He stared at my face. Then he took another two smart steps towards me and stared at me. I wondered why. Then he took another two smart steps so that his face was inches from mine.

'When did you last shave?' he snapped.

'I've never shaved in my life, sir,' I said.

'What?' he gasped, 'never shaved?'

'No, sir,' I said.

'You've got a razor and you've never shaved?' he said.

'No, sir,' I said.

The Sergeant Major turned to a young Corporal with goofy teeth and barked, 'Corporal, take this man and get him shaved.'

I was then marched back to the barrack room by the Corporal. He said, 'Where is your razor, lad?'

'In my kit bag, Corp, but I haven't put a blade in it ' cos I've never shaved!'

The Corporal laughed and got his own razor and said, 'Put up your chin.' He then stroked the razor across my chin and removed one tiny soft hair and blew it off the razor, laughing. I was back on parade within about a couple of minutes and the Sergeant Major looked carefully at my chin and snapped, 'That's better!' My mates tried to resist laughing.

The endless drill, the seemingly pointless fascination with clean boots and kit may seem petty – and often is – but it has a point. As a corporal explained to John Hockey, if a soldier couldn't look after his kit in the barracks, he was going to have a hard time doing it on operations. The aim was to develop, as Vickers realised back in 1917, the self-discipline needed to ensure that every soldier is conditioned to look after himself and his equipment and to take pride in doing so. Collective punishments for those who fail to achieve standards serve to ensure that they work together. Punishments for the squad for an individual's failing drive home the message that a failure by one person will have consequences for them all. Close-order drill, once so important on the battlefield, is still a vital part of the training syllabus. 'Drill, you see,' Captain Peter Jones told the author Tony Parks, 'is designed to teach soldiers to obey orders instinctively and to act as one. Soldiers are much more intelligent today than they used to be: they have to be, because their weapons and equipment are pretty technical pieces of kit. But come the hour and come the day, they still need to have had instilled into them an instinctive obedience to orders. You cannot have debates on the battlefield, you cannot have doubts and hesitations: the soldiers must trust their leaders and do what their leaders say without so much as a second thought.'

The aim of this first stage, says Hockey, is to strip away the individual's civilian attitudes. Major Hayman agrees. '[The] soldier falls into the army way of doing things. These people are maybe two or three weeks out of civilian life.' Very quickly, they leave a civilian attitude behind and focus on becoming a soldier. In what is our society's only formal rite of passage, the young man or woman who completes this first period is rewarded with the presentation of the soldier's beret – a mark of acceptance as a real soldier rather than a civilian.

From here on, Hockey says, training is about learning the skills of the trade, adapting and adjusting to army life. 'The toughest thing a recruit will do,' says Major Hayman, 'is the battle camp at the end of training. It is generally in places like Brecon, in the hills, with the rain and the cold.

They live outside with no cover over their heads, they fight mock battles, and at the end they are totally exhausted. There is one physical task that everybody has to do that is really gut-wrenching. At the end of a 10-mile trek, with battle shooting exercises, you must pick someone up, both of you in full kit, and carry him and his rifle for 100 yards. That is horrendous. If you can get through, you look back and think what a tough guy I am.' Despite its emphasis on obedience, though, he argues that training is not intended to break recruits. 'You don't want to dehumanise them, because you want them to think. A dehumanised human being is no better than a robot. You have to have people who can act on their own when all the officers are dead and the sergeants are gone.' The tasks seem extremely difficult but they are achievable, provided the recruit has the determination to push themselves. 'Pain is temporary,' instructors tell them, 'failure lasts for ever.'

For those who make it, there is one final ceremonial parade at which they are welcomed into the army as fully fledged soldiers. Those who make it go on to join an infantry battalion in the regiment of their choice.

THE REGIMENT

… the British soldier's morale was fed not only by patriotism […]
but by the unique regimental spirit that has been the envy of other
armies down to the present day: one cannot let the Regiment down.

J.M. Brereton, *The British Soldier*

The regimental system of the British army grew out of its role as the enforcement arm of the Empire and has been recognised as being particularly well adapted to small-scale police actions and counterinsurgency operations requiring prolonged deployment away from home. Throughout the Victorian era the army was virtually continuously engaged in low-intensity conflict with insurgents, with full-scale warfare the exception rather than the rule. In such situations, large-scale co-ordination between a number of regiments is rarely necessary and the regiment grew as an independent unit. Each would have at least three battalions: the First deployed overseas; the Second to garrison the UK and provide reinforcements as required; and a Third to act as a Reserve administering training to those men who had completed their full-time service but who remained liable for a part-time Reservist commitment.

'In the old army,' says military historian David Bercuson about the similar system operating in Canada, 'a recruit's service life began in the regimental depot, where he received his basic training and was indoctrinated into his regiment. The process generally took six months and was divided into training and indoctrination. In the words of Colonel Ian Fraser, who commanded the Canadian Airborne Regiment in the mid-1970s, 'It was really a form of brainwashing. The new soldiers memorized battle honours and the names of regimental heroes. They learned about regimental history, ceremonies, customs and traditions, music, bugle calls, order or dress, special drill movements, and all the other trappings that made each regiment in the Canadian Army unique. When they left the depot, the soldiers weren't prepared to admit that any other regiments even existed, much less discuss them with anything other than scorn.'

Most regiments recruited from specific geographical areas and usually incorporated the place name into the regimental name. Each was responsible for its own recruiting, training and administration and this gave each a unique sense of identity to the extent that the British army is often described as tribal. It fosters a strong sense of belonging and often a strong sense of pride and community ownership of the local regiment by the public at home. Inevitably, in times of economic downturn, cuts have to be made. Writing in 1946, Lieutenant Colonel R.J.A. Kaulback noted:

Traditions must be maintained for building up the psychological background of the units, particularly where these traditions are based on recent exploits. For a unit to have fought at Alamein or Arnhem has more military value now than to have fought at Waterloo, however gallant the exploits of those bygone days may have been. Equally, the peculiarities of the modern foot-infantry or the armoured divisions or airborne divisions will engender far greater pride of regiment than perpetuation of the drills of the Fusiliers, Light Infantry or Rifle regiments whose special functions vanished in the twilight of the nineteenth century. Where in the course of reorganization, therefore, the question of amalgamation or disbandment of units comes up for consideration, a very careful choice should be made between those whose retention is desirable on purely sentimental or historical grounds and those whose claim is based on the firmer ground of their record in the recent fighting. There are many very young units whose record should guarantee their place against all claimants in spite of their lack of historical background.

'History suggests,' wrote Major C.E. Hawes in 1951, 'that the British Infantry may fairly claim to be second to none in staunchness and fortitude in battle: until recently at any rate regimental spirit was the characteristic feature of that infantry, every member of which was determined that his regiment should hold its ground regardless of what its neighbours might do. Is it too paradoxical to claim therefore that the success of British Infantry has been based upon the principle "Divided we stand"? The value of regimental tradition also appears in its affects upon leadership. Here again the commander of the more technical arms has an advantage; the most important part of his task is the application of principles, scientifically established and agreed upon, to a given situation which may indeed be affected by the fact that it occurs in time of war but is not radically altered thereby. Thus, in peace or war, it takes very little time for a seaman with any experience at all to sum up a new Captain [...] Similarly it is very soon clear whether a commander of artillery or engineers is technically competent. But the command of infantry in action is far more closely allied to an art than to a technique: it consists of the application of principles, it is true, but these principles are profoundly modified by the individual commander's view of the way to apply them, in fact, by his personal character. Thus a thrusting Irishman may attack with three companies up, while a cautious Scot may prefer to commit only one company at the outset: both may succeed admirably, but it is probable that neither will have much success at all unless he has somehow gained the confidence of his men before the battle, so that every soldier will go "all out" without anxious fears of something going wrong. Such confidence is based on knowledge, and knowledge is more easily and quickly acquired if both leader and led are on the same metaphorical "wavelength" as the result of a common military culture and upbringing based on shared traditions.'

So great is this sense of tribal loyalty to a specific regiment that it is not unusual to hear a teenage Guardsman today talk of how 'We held the line' when talking about the battle of Waterloo or any of the many other battle honours of the regiment. The pride in regimental history remains so strong that even the lowest recruit gains a sense of ownership of a distant historical event. They were Guardsmen, he's a Guardsman, therefore there is no doubt in his mind that he, too, would behave the same way. Within the regiment, the basic unit for most of a soldier's army life will be the Battalion. Varying between 700 and 900 men and commanded by a Lieutenant Colonel, 'battalions certainly differed in their character and their competence both from others and within themselves over time,' noted Terry Copp and Bill McAndrew in their study of the army of World War II. 'Battalions are much like an organic family. They are held together by intangibles – leadership, comradeship, motivation, morale – that defy quantification or even easy description. In good units, soldiers feel – know – they are in the best section in the best company, in the best battalion. Many veterans cite the character and capability of the commanding officer as vital factors in shaping a battalion's collective character.'

Jeffery Williams, in his account of World War I, noted an incident that demonstrated the bond between the men of a battalion:

Message: 'German attack east of St. Eloi … relief postponed.' That extra sentence seemed a lot to men who had not slept for five days and there was some cursing in the darkness. Colonel Farquhar, following his usual custom of considering the front line as healthy as a village lane, appeared at the back of the trench.

'And how is the merry band of sportsmen?' he remarked cheerfully. No one had heard or noticed his approach, but the replies were ready enough.

'Going strong, sir.'

'Good for another week.'

'Enjoying ourselves, sir.'

The colonel chuckled and departed while the men looked at each other and wondered why they had answered that way. But really there was no other.

In a speech to officer candidates at Sandhurst, Sergeant-Major J.C. Lord tried to explain what this sense of belonging meant:

I am going to relate to you something that happened to me that I think highlights this business. In my parachute battalion we had a Corporal Sheriff. He was a good corporal but he had his share of rockets and so on. He didn't make sergeant when there was plenty of promotion flying about but he was a good battalion [man] and a good company man. He joined us in '41, fought with us in North Africa, Sicily and Italy and finally at Arnhem, and it was at Arnhem that he was wounded. We had been in the prison camp for I should think about three months with no knowledge of him at all when I was told that he was in the reception hut, and so I scrounged a few cigarettes which were available, because I was told he was in bad shape, and went up to the hut.

I shall never forget it. As I opened the door everything stopped: there was a deathly silence and everybody looked round as they do under those circumstances. The hut was full of foreigners of various nationalities, a smell of unwashed bodies and a strange atmosphere. I looked around and saw Corporal Sheriff in some strange uniform – if you could call it a uniform – which had been supplied to him. He was sitting cross-legged on the floor, head hanging down, looking very dejected.

I walked across towards him and you could have heard a pin drop. I went up to him and I said something to the effect, 'Hello Corporal Sheriff, how are you getting on?' And in front of all those foreigners he stood up. It was three months since we had seen one another and he had no particular cause to love me. In front of all those foreigners he stood up and he stood to attention and you could almost hear their astonishment.

He turned his head towards me and said, 'Hello Sir, it's good to hear your voice.' He was blind. Even in those circumstances he was a member of the family, he felt he belonged again and he was back in the bosom of the family. Now that's soldiering, that's spirit, that's understanding. That's all the things I've been trying to say.

Today, the regimental system has been eroded. Regiments with strong local connections have been amalgamated and training is no longer carried out by individual regiments but in generic training centres. The traditions of the past remain strong but have given way to a more corporate set of values.

'Being a soldier is not easy,' says the army's website in 2010. 'We are asked to do things not asked of other people. We have to be aggressive and strong in battle, yet behave properly and show self-control all the time. To enable us to do this the Army has six values it requires us to live by.

Selfless Commitment

The Army is about teamwork – none of us work on our own, we always work in a team. Teams can only be effective if we all play our part in full, putting the team and the mission before our own needs, trusting each other totally – even with our lives if necessary.

Courage

All soldiers need courage, both physical and moral. Physical courage is about controlling fear, rather than having no fear. Training and discipline helps us do our duty regardless of the dangers and discomforts. Moral courage is about doing the right thing, not looking the other way when we know or see something is wrong, even if it is not a popular thing to do or say.

Discipline

All teams need discipline. In our line of work it is vital, ensuring that orders are carried out and everyone is confident that they will not be let down by their teammates. Self-discipline is the best form of discipline. It depends on high personal standards that earn soldiers the trust and respect of their teammates. It gives us the courage to make the difficult choices that we face in our career.

Integrity

Integrity means being honest, not lying, cheating or stealing. If we lack integrity our teammates cannot trust what we say or do; they cannot rely on us and the team suffers.

Loyalty

Loyalty is about looking after and helping those around us. Putting the needs of our teammates before our own, even when the going gets tough.

Respect For Others

Soldiers come in all shapes and sizes and all deserve to be treated fairly. There is no place for any form of harassment or discrimination in an Army that claims to 'Be The Best.' We judge people on their abilities, not their race, religion or sex. Respect for others, including civilians, detainees and captured enemy forces, means treating people decently.

Hundreds of books have been dedicated to the task of explaining Tommy Atkins, who he is, why he fights. There is no simple answer. Perhaps the best summary of the modern British soldier comes from Private Kenny Bosch of 7 Platoon, C Company of 1st Battalion, Princess of Wales' Royal Regiment, nicknamed 'the Tigers'. Interviewed by Professor Richard Holmes about his experiences in Iraq, Bosch explained:

The search for yourself leads you on many paths through your life. Some are long and hard, while others are as short as a heartbeat. But the moment you think you have found yourself, the search starts all over again. For as you find yourself you change and become a better man [...] And then it happens, your first contact. You come face-to-face with the demon inside you. Fear and anxiety grips you and squeezes the very life out of you. This is life and death. This is where a man stands up and faces his destiny. This is what you have been training for. This is what you were born for. You were born to be a warrior. You were born to be strong and courageous; to be a man. And with that the demon turns and runs. The fear and anxiety disappears and your senses sharpen to a knife's edge with which you take control of yourself and lunge forward. You look round and you see the eyes of the man next to you. You grow strong with the confidence you see in their faces. For a split second you almost feel sorry for the foes that stumble in the way of a force like this.

But a man is more than just a warrior, and war is more than just fighting battles. After all, we came to keep the peace [...] Peace starts with you, as a soldier, walking the streets, talking to people. To give a little bit of who you are and what you know so that they may have a better life. This is something you cannot train for. The life you live in the battalion is the one that shines through you. As you give, you also receive. What you get back is what changes you [...] The only ones that understand you are the people who were there with you. The ones who have seen what you have seen and experienced what you have experienced.

So where does all of this leave me? Have I become a man? Did my training prepare me mentally? I am left with the most profound statement I have heard about being who you are, and spoken by one of my childhood heroes, Popeye the Sailor Man. Whenever he wasn't sure what to do or felt inadequate, Popeye would simply say, 'I yam what I yam'. Today I can truly say, I yam what I yam. I am a soldier in the best armoured infantry battalion in the world. I am a Tiger.

CHAPTER THREE
START LINE

Noun: a real or imaginary line, the crossing of which marks the start of an advance, attack or other offensive operation.
Abbreviation SL. See also 'line of departure.'

www.militarydictionary.com

Every military operation has its own start line and once across it, there is no going back. It marks the point of no return. Every individual, though, has their own start line. It is that moment when you know that things have irrevocably changed. You are no longer a peacetime soldier, playing at war. What you do from now on may get you killed. It's a hard line to cross for all kinds of reasons.

In May 1940 the German army was sweeping through France. After nine months of the 'Phoney War', a British armoured column was sent to attack the enemy flank at Arras. As it advanced, the column arrived at a level crossing on the D60 Dainville–Achicourt road. The barrier was down. After years of exercises in which every effort was made to avoid any damage to private property because the army simply couldn't afford the costs of compensation, the column ground to a halt. It was some time before anyone plucked up the courage to smash through.

'Don't you know there's a war on?' was a familiar enough expression during World War II, yet it captured perfectly the air of unreality that often accompanies war. On a bright summer's day it can be almost impossible to believe that the ships out at sea and the men walking past are engaged in a struggle to the death. Max Hastings, accompanying the Falklands Task Force, remembers finding islanders watching a video as all around them the British army and navy fought a war. The video? A war film.

The men who dropped from the sky or waded ashore in Normandy had been at war since the day they were called up and mentally ready since their call-up papers arrived. For those who have experienced peacetime soldiering, setting out for war can be an odd business. 'There was a lot of pomp and ceremony as we left Southampton,' recalls Falklands veteran Denzil Connick. 'As we boarded the ship, the Parachute Regiment Band and the Band of the Royal Marines played. All our families were there, flying flags and waving us off. As the ship sailed away, we could see people lining the coastal roads in their cars, flashing their lights and beeping their horns, but as the coastline disappeared the mood on the ship changed. It went very quiet and thoughtful. My thoughts were: "Will I ever see Britain again? Will I be coming back?" As we sailed towards Ascension Island, the soldiers aboard the ship spent every minute practising their military skills and getting their fitness up to scratch. We still weren't sure that we would actually see any action. The feeling was that we would probably just arrive and the diplomats would have sorted it out. But then we heard that the *Belgrano* had been sunk and we knew there was no going back.'

Journalists Robert McGowan and Jeremy Hands sailed with the Falklands Task Force in 1982: 'Somehow, [passing] Sierra Leone marked the end of the holiday, the point where the serious intentions began. The pervading feeling of "tee hee, bet we never get there" suddenly changed to one of "Jesus, we really are going all the way."' Aboard the luxury liners commandeered to transport troops, ship's stewards wore helmets as they served tea and coffee in the lounges.

American psychiatrist Dr J. Dowling's term 'apprehensive enthusiasm' is a good summary of most soldiers' emotions during the period leading up to their first experience of combat. It encapsulates the strange mixture of dread, disbelief and sheer excitement. Each soldier looks ahead and wonders what sort of person he or she will become as they face the ultimate test. Many set off on the road to battle conscious of the fact that they are about to embark upon an experience which, for good or ill, is unique. Roy Grinker and John Speigel described how men fantasise about the upcoming experience: 'Their minds are full of romanticized, Hollywood versions of their future activities in combat, coloured with vague ideas of being a hero and winning ribbons and decorations for startling exploits and with all sorts of exhibitionist fantasies to which few would publicly admit.' Will they do their duty or will they fail? As Lieutenant Alan Hanbury-Sparrow wrote as he went to war in August 1914: 'What's all the knowledge of the world compared with what we are about to discover?'

Author Raleigh Trevelyan recalled his 'father saying to me on embarkation leave that the worst part of battle was wondering how you were going to behave in front of other people [...] I don't think even now I really fear death, or even the process of dying. It is only the thought of whether or not I shall acquit myself honourably that obsesses me.' Quietly, troops look inside themselves and think about the future. Between closest friends, soldiers talk about their fears of being seriously wounded. Secretly, some make pacts with the man they trust most: 'If things look really bad, you will put an end to it for me, won't you?' From time to time, the promise has to be kept.

Ian Gardiner, a company commander in the Royal Marines during the Falklands, remembers: 'It is not easy to describe one's feelings before one is committed to battle. Fear, certainly, plays a part but it is not fear of death itself. It is more a sadness for the grief that will follow one's death among one's family. As a company commander responsible for the lives of some 150 men, I felt pretty lonely in that hour when our preparations were complete and before we moved off, but I am prepared to bet that each individual felt just as lonely in his own way. I found that I didn't actually want anyone to speak to me. I spent my hour smoking a cigar and preparing myself to accept whatever disasters the night might bring – in a single word – praying. It was a mental exercise I would not care to have to repeat.'

For some, the journey to the combat zone may take weeks by ship. For others it may be just a few hours by plane. All too soon, though, the day dawns when the soldier arrives 'in theatre'. Their war is about to start. Whatever the fantasies that have built up on the way, the reality is often very different.

'We'd been messed about,' former Paratrooper Jim Love remembers about his arrival on the Falklands.

Just like the Grand Old Duke of York's troops. Up the stairs, down the stairs, and back round to start again. Tonight it was a bit different though, after this practice we weren't going back to our cabins. We were assembling in the forward lounge for a final briefing. A church service of sorts was also being held by the padre, David Cooper. It was totally voluntary attendance, of course.

I went because I had only got around to paying him the twenty pounds that I owed him. It was for conducting my wedding service at the Garrison church in Aldershot. They'd given me four hours off to get married. When it came to paying for the service and organist I was skint. So the padre kindly offered to pay. It didn't pay to be on the wrong side of the line in circumstances such as these.

The forward lounge had a tinge of religion attached to it. We must have sat in it watching Monty Python's the *Life of Brian* God only knows how many times. The song 'Always Look On The Bright Side of Life' had become a bit of a theme tune for the whole adventure. It was, however, quite pleasant to see how many people had found religion in the last few hours before the dawn on 21 May. A couple of mumbled verses of 'To Be a Pilgrim' were duly sung and Padre Cooper gave us the good word. Then it was all down to us.

We were all professional soldiers trained to an extremely high standard. Supremely confident in our own abilities to cope with any given situation. With an absolute faith in our comrades that they would be there with us, shoulder to shoulder. It was the politicians we couldn't trust, [but we all felt] it didn't hurt to have an extra bit of air cover from really high up if the shit hit the fan.

I'd actually missed the only practice run at filling the LCU [landing craft]. That had taken place several days before at Ascension Island. It had been a bit too hot and bright. I'd been suffering from a hangover at the time. I had managed to find some excuse to get out of the practice. Quite lucky really, because they had ended going round and round the bay for a couple of hours. A couple of the blokes had managed to top up their tans and the rest got heat stroke.

It had been a trip round the bay in reality. Shorts, PT vests, sunshades and life jackets. There only being twenty life jackets, hence only twenty people on each trip. It was a real eye opener when it finally happened for real. No life jackets, total darkness and an attempt at the f*cking world record for filling an LCU with overladen troops. It took hours. I honestly can't remember if it was cold that morning or not. It was crisp, but I never felt the cold.

Fortunately we didn't have to climb down any scramble nets or such like. It would have probably been a physical impossibility I reckon anyway. No. It was simply what you might say, 'a blind leap of faith' into the darkness. Into what you hoped would be the arms of someone to help drag you across the side of the LCU. To safety. Well, what was considered the relative safety of the bobbing-like-a-cork craft. (It was better than drowning of course.) Nobody wanted to end up in the cold embrace of the South Atlantic and Davy Jones' locker.

When it was apparent that they couldn't get any more in the LCU we set sail in a circular course until they managed to fill the other two LCUs. Then it was off to the landing site of Blue Beach 2. We did have one well wisher who waved us bon voyage. Wendy [the gay ship's crewman who had organised shows and entertainment throughout the voyage] had decided to say goodbye to us all and wish us luck. The total darkness of the South Atlantic was split by a ray of light from the upper decks of the *Norland* when Wendy opened one of the deck doors. It was like a searchlight. We could actually hear him calling 'Bye boys' in the eerie silence above the LCU's engine. Over a hundred voices in unison told him to 'shut the f*cking door'. And he did.

The plan was that the SBS would secure the landing site and if it was all clear they would show a green light. If a red light was seen then it was a hot beach and the enemy were waiting for us. No lights and it probably meant we were in the wrong place. Squashed in like we were, face stuck in the Bergen of the man in front. I had visions of the film *The Longest Day*. High cliff faces, men being machine gunned and shelled while trying to wade ashore. They didn't have the heavy Bergens that we had, however. They also had forgot to tell us what the beach would be like. We could hear the hooligans [SAS] on Fanning Head as we passed in the dark waters below.

I don't know how long it took. Time wasn't a factor. We did, however, fail to find any lights on the first two attempts to beach (it being decided after each abortive attempt that we were in the wrong place). On the third try, we managed to reach a decision in the wheel house that this was it. With the engine putt-putting away, the LCU crunched and scraped its way towards the rocky beach. The closer we got, the more the tension increased in the middle and rear section of the LCU. This was due to not being able to see anything except the bloke in front of you – or rather his Bergen. Messages were passed from man to man, forward and back again in whispered tones.

'Can you see a light?'

'No.'

'Can you see the beach?'

'No.'

'Can you see anything?'

'No. Some f*cker's put a big metal ramp where the window should be.'

They decided to drop the ramp anyway.

There came the cry 'Ramp down troops out'. This was it, the retaking of the islands. The invasion was on. Nothing happened. It was repeated. Still nothing happened. Nobody moved. One of the crew of the LCU scrambled along the side of the craft to the front and the ramp.

'What's up?' whispered the tentative voice of the Marine.

'Have you seen how deep the f*cking water is, take us in a bit closer,' came the reply.

'Get out.'

'F*ck off.'

The CSM intervened, he started shouting, 'Go! Go! Go!'

Men started to move. The invasion was back on again.

Soon it was my turn. I stepped off the end of the ramp and into the chin-deep, ball-breaking icy waters of the South Atlantic. I was relatively lucky – I'm 6'2". The bloke in front had been about 5'6". All I saw was a helmet bobbing towards the shore in front of me.

We sloshed ashore across a small two-foot wide pebble beach. Then climbed the foot-high bank on to dry soil. Everybody was milling about. There appeared to be no enemy positions or any sign in fact, that they were even there. The invasion stopped for a moment yet again.

Everybody needed a piss.

Once that had been sorted we set about finding where everybody was and formed up in our respective groups. Two of the officers appeared to be arguing with a couple of nuns. You could see the out lines of figures in black with a light or white ring around the face. Similar to the nun's habit. I'm glad I never said hello sister, cause it was the SBS blokes. Apparently they weren't very happy, because they weren't expecting us for another two nights yet. We offered to go home again. They didn't laugh.

We moved off along the coastline following a narrow path. Heading towards our second objective, Sussex Mountains. Most of us would never feel that we had dried out at any stage after that first soaking. Especially our boots and feet.

Twenty-six years earlier, Marine David Henderson had experienced similar confusion when he landed at Suez:

As we neared Port Said we were all prepared for the landing wearing light fighting gear only (our Bergens with our spare kit and K rations were to follow us later). It was true they followed us but somebody forgot to pass on the information that we were not attacking the harbour by landing craft now but hitting the beach by helicopter. As a result our gear was put ashore in the wrong place and we had very little to eat the whole day [...] On top of our normal supply of personal ammo we carried quantities of mortar bombs, Energa grenades and spare mags for the Bren guns, spread out evenly amongst us. All in all quite a load. We were not allowed on deck until our turn to load up and this did not help our nerves one bit. We could hear the sounds of shelling and bombs going off for what seemed hours and I must admit that my brain was whirring with all kinds of thoughts. At last our squad was summoned on deck and we made our way up narrow stairs and passageways loaded down and bumping into everything on the way.

Strangely, as soon as we came out into daylight all fear seemed to leave us for the moment and we clustered at the ship's rail staring at the sight of the British and French invasion fleet. It was incredible – there were craft of every shape and size all around us, and some were already making their way back into station having unloaded their men and material somewhere ashore, while others were offloading still more into smaller landing craft.

A huge pall of heavy black smoke was pouring skyward from some fuel depot that had either been shelled or bombed and one or two large buildings were also alight. There was also a continuous thump and whine of gun fire as escort ships laid down a pattern of fire well inland of the troops who were already ashore. There were no helicopters on deck, so we assumed they were somewhere on the beach delivering squads of our buddies, so we were directed to our marked out positions as practised and waited. Soon we could see the craft approaching, not in well-formed formations, but strung out at irregular intervals and different heights and it was apparent that at this stage of the operations the pilots were not in the least interested in pretty flying but just getting in and out with their loads and trusting the opposition were lousy shots.

Our craft came thumping down onto the deck and we all scrambled aboard and held on for the expected lurch as we took off, but instead we watched as the pilots and crew calmly got off and stood around chatting or walked around stretching their legs. One or two high-ranking officers came over and engaged the pilots in animated conversation and made some sort of notes on maps as they had, of course, been receiving constant reports over the radio, but I suppose there was nothing to match face-to-face reporting. After what seemed ages the crew climbed aboard and with an escalating roar of engines we were on our way. At this point my bowels hinted that I had better not open my legs too much or they might just cause me a bit of embarrassment. Nobody spoke, nobody looked at one another; we had all picked a far-off point either out the door or on the floor and just stared.

'Out! Out! Out!' screamed a voice from somewhere, and like an elephant relieving itself after a particularly heavy meal we poured out the door of the craft landing on top of one another and spread out on the sand. Off went our transport in what seemed a rather hasty exit and as it made its way back for its next bundle of nervous men with the sound of its engines slowly diminishing, we became aware of the sounds of outgoing and incoming small arms fire.

I checked my rear end area and was relieved to find that the overwhelming explosion that had happened to me as my feet hit the beach had only been wind. Our sergeant and corporal marshalled us together and we moved up to form a line along a promenade wall where we laid out our forward markers (this was a series of vivid coloured strips that troops would lay out indicating to any supporting fighter plane the forward positions we had reached). This had hardly been finished when there was a terrifying scream of engines and a blur of explosions as one of our own Navy attack fighters did a strafing run straight up the beach. It has never been explained to me how a pilot supporting a beach landing that had been progressing for some time could possibly think to track his run straight along the water's edge. Thankfully no one in our squad was hit but many boys in a following wave of choppers caught the brunt of the attack and two of them were lads I had gone through basic training with. After the shock of this, and probably because of it, what happened next was straight out of some *Carry On* film. We were all lined up behind this wall fearfully taking in the area in front of us over which we were getting ready to move.

Over the road was a line of buildings, mostly blocks of flats, which were all linked together by a wall with one or two gates in it, and we were all squinting at the doors and windows straining to catch a sight of the enemy. Nothing moved and we were sure that with all the activity on the beach, any defenders would have moved back. Suddenly, a figure holding a rifle appeared as if from nowhere right in front of us and began to trot along the length of this wall. Without waiting, we all opened up on him blazing away with great gusto. He stopped dead in his tracks and stared at us and without thinking we also stopped firing. Then he was off again this time as fast as his feet could go and off we went again firing at him with a trail of bullet holes following his track and dust flying all around him. He must have been very good at his prayers that morning because not one of us hit him and he scampered round the end of the buildings and out of sight. Our sergeant by this time was going crazy stamping his feet in the sand and crying out for us to cease fire and take aim all at the same time.

Once he got us under control we got the bollocking of our lives, and this was not the type of lecture we had screamed at us by our instructors during training, this was meant to be understood and we certainly got the message, from the fact that we were wasting precious ammunition right up to his last statement of, 'Shooting the next bastard who let off wasted shots.' I often wonder if some Egyptian officer was watching the beach through his binoculars trying to work out what tactic was being planned with this squad of Marines sitting in a row on the sand with an NCO lecturing and waving his hands about. It was a different set of men who crossed the road after that incident, as nothing beats reality for teaching someone the facts of life; you didn't stop somebody by just pointing your rifle in his general direction and pulling the trigger, you forced yourself to get control of your fear and take aim. Very difficult but a life saver.

Once the soldier has landed in the war zone, he quickly finds himself somewhere that American military historian S.L.A. Marshall once described as the loneliest place where men could be together. Even in the sectors of the World War I Western Front where the trenches were only metres apart, men could go for months without seeing a live German. Even in the midst of some of the greatest battles of the war, soldiers never saw the enemy except as a distant blur. Men talk about 'the empty battlefield' because it's a brave or foolish soldier who, knowing the enemy is somewhere out there, stands up. For the most part the infantryman's world is limited to the few yards on either side of his position and at ground level. Studies conducted amongst the American military in World War II found that men in these isolated positions, unable to really see what is happening, often took no part in battle, even when their lines were under attack. Only specialists and men who worked in teams to man machine guns, mortars and bazookas routinely reacted aggressively. For many, the experience of suddenly having another human being attempt to kill you is almost too surreal to accept.

In a blog from Afghanistan, Lance Corporal James Atkin of 21 Engineer Regiment wrote about his first 'contact':

The task was to clear an 8km route to a patrol base. I have worked with the four men on the team in the past but never on a search task [searching for booby traps and hidden roadside bombs]. Off to the right of us was a steady hill with small compounds scattered 400m away along the side of the hill. There were people walking around by the compounds, and there was some greenery up there. Off to the left about 300m away were cornfields. So I was enjoying my time on this mission with the views and scenery. It was disgustingly hot and the ground was baking hard sand. Behind our team was a fleet of vehicles. The machines are huge, angry-looking, rumbling things with big heavy guns constantly looking around for any threats. I felt pretty safe in this environment despite the country I am in. The search team I was working with was commanded by Lance Corporal 'Mick' Meagan who is cool, calm and methodical. The other three searchers I knew I could trust as much as I can trust myself. So that is the scene set.

So, we were walking along doing our thing, making sure that our path was clear of any improvised explosive devices [IEDs]. Just minding our own business. When out of the corner of my eye I saw some puffs of sand jump up, maybe thirty metres away. Then I heard the gunshots. Four or five of them. I stood there for a split second and asked out aloud, 'Are we being shot at?' I looked at the others but they were already down on their belt buckles. I kept my eyes on the target as I hit the ground and the baddie ran into the compound he was stood next to. The range to the target outweighed the distance that my pistol could shoot at. Messages were shouted back. The gunners in the vehicles trained their weapons on the compound. But children quickly came back out to play and life went back to normal by the compounds. So we would have been prevented from shooting even if the guy had reappeared. We ran back to the safe haven behind the trucks and eventually clambered into the lead armoured truck. That was it, the contact ended.

Now I smile to myself and realise I can tell people I have been in the thick of the action, and I will spend my spare time working on my thousand-yard stare. Others claim that it wasn't even a contact as we didn't shoot back. I think they are just jealous. It was the first time anyone has shot at the men and women of 15 Squadron. It was also the first time in my eight years in the Army I have been shot at. It was nothing compared to the rest of the gun battles we hear about from other regiments but it was still interesting. It is a story I'll not tell my mum.

Serving in Borneo, Keith Scott's experience was very different to the random shots aimed at Corporal Atkin:

The confrontation years in Borneo can quite rightly be said to be one of Britain's small and 'dirty' guerrilla wars. Any engagements that did take place tended to be rather fleeting affairs, where usually the maximum amount of time spent in a 'firefight' was probably no more than a few minutes. Although there were occasions when longer engagements took place between larger, more evenly matched and equally determined forces. My own part in all this was usually concerned with the hit and run and dirty tricks tactics, classic components of guerrilla warfare and a little less on more involved fighting. My first experience of being under fire, though, was a very real in-your-face baptism, up close (about 30 feet) and very personal. It wasn't a few random shots fired roughly in the direction of myself and my comrades, the opposition were making a determined attempt to kill each one of us. When I had time to catch a breath, I found I had wet myself in fear, and Christ knows how, but I had also managed to eat a whole tube of sweets all at once without taking the individual wrappers off. I was 21 then, and my hair started going grey quite quickly after that. By the time I was 28 I had a head of hair the colour of an old man's, like it is now. But it can't all have been down to chance, not after escaping that amount of times – physically at least.

It's at this moment of first contact that a soldier learns what sort of person he is. He can either react or die. Only he can decide which it is to be. In his poetry, Jim Love has drawn on his own experiences of having to make a lonely decision under fire. Here he explains the background to it:

I was just bimbling along, brain in neutral, when all of a sudden some bastard turned the lights on. Now lots of people will say that a tracer is pretty impressive and is a wondrous sight to behold. But I'll tell you people, when it's coming towards you and you can see every one of them coming, believe me, it puts the shits right up you! Death is now staring you right in the face. Bodies fell over like skittles. Right/left/right. I went forward and down, facedown. My chest and elbows hit the ground. Then my face hit. It smashed into the grass and mud and into the sheep shit. I tried to lift my head up and get my face out of the shit – literally.

I couldn't move, panic started to set in. I used my elbows for leverage, I moved a little then was face down again. My God I'd been hit! It was the only reasonable explanation. But where? I couldn't feel any pain, no holes. It's the shock, my brain told me. You won't feel anything because of the shock, the pain will hit you later. Right, I've got to find out where the wound is before I lose what strength I've got and I'm not able to move at all.

I rolled to my left. It wasn't easy. A couple of flies buzzed past my head. I looked up, to my right. It was like one of those cartoons on TV. Where the gopher or Bugs Bunny digs a tunnel across the golf course greens. Little bits of grass and mud were leaping in the air just like on TV, amazing.

Then I saw my antenna, the top section and at least half of the next section was stuck into the ground. That's why I couldn't move, stupid bastard. I hadn't been shot, it was the radio. The smack I'd felt that split second after I'd hit the deck was the weight of the radio slamming into me. I giggled, chuffed to f*ck. What now? That was the question. I looked back to where the tracer had been doing its Bugs Bunny impersonations. Nobody was moving, the tracer continued its sweep left.

Suddenly, one of the skittles leapt up from where he'd been lying and started to zig-zag, bobbing and weaving. I willed him on – crazy bastard, you're going to die. He jigged right, mad bastard, run for it. Yes … I promised to myself if he makes 15 metres, I'll get up and go too. The tracer had stopped and switched. Homing in on him, yellow/white flashes of light slicing through the still morning air. There still hadn't been any noise up till now, just the flies. There did seem to be a lot of flies about though, it must have been the sheep shit. 'Well', I thought. 'If he makes 30 metres, I'll definitely go for it.' While I'd been watching, I'd slid backwards and managed to free my antenna.

The runner went down, the tracer was zooming over his head. I stopped breathing. Everything stopped. I could visualise the Argy gunner on tip toes, looking over the breech, beyond the barrel, to see if he'd got one.

He hadn't. Skittle number one was crawling like hell towards a fold in the ground. He rolled into the dip and was gone from sight. I was up and lumbering forward. Bodies were moving in a multitude of directions. One thoroughly pissed-off Argy machine-gunner started up again but it was like swatting at a fly on a table top. And he'd missed! Now the air was thick with flies and he didn't know which one to go for. 'Not me!' my brain screamed, 'not me! pick somebody else.' I was doing well, there was some thick yellow gorse ahead of me. The childish element had re-entered my brain once again. The gorse will hide you! Go for the gorse. Don't be silly; it's sharp, and spiky as hell. I could hurt myself.

The radio. If I go in backwards, using the weight of the radio in my Bergen, it'll take me right through the middle of the gorse bush and out of sight. Yes. A f*cking excellent idea. Let's do it. I had actually managed to build a bit of speed up as it happened. I suppose a little bit of adrenalin and a lot of fear does that to you. I half leapt, semi-spun into the air as I got close to the gorse. I tried to hold my head up but my back was arching. Like they used to teach you at school. The Fosbury Flop high jump technique of the seventies. It wasn't style. It was the weight of the radio in my Bergen, pulling me down. I hit the gorse. I bounced. Then I bounced again. I thrashed my arms and legs. Nothing. I just thrashed. I lay there, like a stranded turtle, on a posture sprung mattress. Bobbing up and down. The tracer swung my way. I did the only thing I could: I laughed. I couldn't do anything else. I think the laughter was just changing to racking great sobs 'cause I was really starting to lose it when the top branches snapped and I fell through the bush.

I reckon that the Argy machine-gunner must have been laughing his bollocks off too. He missed, and it all went high and over the top. Reality had set back in once more. I was yet again in the shit (sheep of course). The soft stuff stank to high heaven but the hardened pellets dug into my knees. I was crawling along a tunnel (obviously made by the local sheep) about as fast as a man can who has just tried to hide behind a prominent yellow gorse bush – from several hundred individuals armed with machine guns which could demolish the proverbial brick shithouse wall in under five minutes. What a dick. I just hoped none of the lads saw me, they'd take the piss for a week if they had.

I looked around to see how many others had made it to safety at the bottom of the steep incline that was known as Darwin Hill. After a quick check, I came to the conclusion that there was only me. With my back to the hill, the sea was on my right, and nobody else. To my left was where the bad men were, and that's an understatement. (Later described as poor little conscripts, who were mistreated and underfed. Not from where I had been sitting.) Perhaps they've already started up the hill without me. 'Right,' I thought, 'nothing for it, I'll have to go up the hill. No cover after I leave here though, could be a bit of a problem. Crawl. Now there's an idea, brilliant one, too.' So, I started to crawl up the slope armed with my radio and my trusty 9mm Sterling Sub-Machine gun. After God only knows how long I noticed I was getting quite near to the summit. Which meant I was going to be seen by just about everybody on the island. I would also probably have to stand up. Quite honestly, I was f*cking knackered. I stopped for a rest and looked over to my right, from where there was quite a lot of smoke and, on the wind, the sound of heavy small arms fire.

However, there wasn't anyone really close to me. In fact, checking the left flank brought the same conclusion. I was on my own. Right. I checked my [ammo magazine], and made sure the breech wasn't obstructed, got ready to get up and do a one-man assault for the top of the hill. Then I had a better plan. I was on my own up here. At least there were lots of people on the right flank. There was a hell of a fire fight going on. I crawled off to my right and started back down the hill, towards the smoke and the firefight. If I was going to die, I was not going to do it on my own. I wanted to at least see a friendly face. Someone I knew. I went off to find the lads.

CHAPTER FOUR
CLOSE TO HOME

Today, in Northern Ireland, another soldier ...

Operation Banner 1969–1998

The Queen has been graciously pleased to approve the posthumous award of the George Cross to:
2391067 Sergeant Michael WILLETTS, The Parachute Regiment.

At 8.24pm on the evening of 25 May 1971, a terrorist entered the reception hall of the Springfield Road Police Station in Belfast. He carried a suitcase from which a smoking fuse protruded, dumped it quickly on the floor and fled outside. Inside the room were a man and a woman, two children and several police officers. One of the latter saw at once the smoking case and raised the alarm. The Police Officers began to organise the evacuation of the hall past the reception desk, through the reception office and out by a door into the rear passage.

Sergeant Michael Willetts was on duty in the inner hall. Hearing the alarm, he sent an NCO up to the first floor to warn those above and hastened himself to the door through which a police officer was thrusting those in the reception hall and office. He held the door open while all passed safely through and then stood in the doorway, shielding those taking cover. In the next moment, the bomb exploded with terrible force.

Sergeant Willetts was mortally wounded. His duty did not require him to enter the threatened area, for his post was elsewhere. He knew well, after 4 months service in Belfast, the peril of going towards a terrorist bomb but he did not hesitate to do so. All those approaching the door from the far side agree that if they had had to check to open the door they would have perished. Even when they had reached the rear passage, Sergeant Willetts waited, placing his body as a screen to shelter them. By this considered act of bravery, he risked – and lost – his life for those of the adults and children. His selflessness, his courage are beyond praise.

London Gazette, 21 June 1971

Born in 1943, after leaving school Michael Willetts worked in a local colliery near his home in Nottinghamshire before joining the British army, where he volunteered for the Parachute Regiment and was posted to the 3rd Battalion. During his time in the army he married Sandra and the couple had two children, Dean and Trudy. After promotion to Sergeant, Willetts, a Catholic, was deployed with the battalion to Northern Ireland at the outbreak of violence there between Irish Nationalist and British Unionist communities in 1971. On 25 May, a man in his mid-twenties emerged from a car and threw a suitcase containing a blast bomb into the lobby of the Royal Ulster Constabulary station on the Springfield Road. Seven RUC officers, two British soldiers and eighteen civilians were injured in the attack and Willetts himself fatally injured by a chunk of metal from a locker which had struck him in the back of the head. As he and the rest of the wounded were being carried from the building, local crowds gathered to cheer the IRA 'victory' and taunt the survivors. He died after two hours on the operating table at the Royal Victoria Hospital in Belfast.

Folk singer Harvey Andrews used the story as the basis for his song 'Soldier', saying, in the sleeve notes to his album *Writer of Songs*, 'If you can con an ordinary man into protecting your interests, he gets done when the crisis comes, not you. Many soldiers are not professional killers, they're kids who couldn't get a job, and as unemployment has soared, recruiting for the army has increased by over 60% in three years. The average soldier is unimportant in the final analysis, it's the ones who shelter behind him that count [...] and they always seem to survive!' Despite this, Andrews found himself heavily criticised for having written a pro-establishment glorification of military heroism. As Roy Palmer, author of a study of soldiers' songs explained, 'Harvey Andrews was so struck by the incident that he wrote the song to make the point that soldiers, too, are human. (The incident of the soldier's embracing the bomb was poetic licence.) Broadcasts of Andrews' record were banned for some time by the BBC lest feelings be exacerbated in the nationalist community of Northern Ireland. The Ministry of Defence advised (and still advises) soldiers not to sing the song in pubs where it might cause trouble. Some have interpreted this as a ban. Nevertheless, they sing it "all the time", according to one source, on military transport and in messes and canteens. It has been said that some units require newcomers to learn to sing or recite the song before they become fully accepted.'

It was a song that spoke for generations of young men, many not even born when Willetts died, who would follow him onto the streets of Belfast during the 30 years of Operation Banner.

When British troops were first deployed to Northern Ireland, many were welcomed by the Catholic population, who for years had been intimidated and attacked by both loyalists and rogue elements of the RUC. One former member of the Royal Regiment of Wales recalls being on patrol on the Springfield Road when they 'heard shouts and whacking noises coming from another street, so we legged it over there and we seen two men in black uniforms hitting this woman with what looked like a hockey stick and the other fellow had a big stick and they was smacking this woman as she lay on the floor. They stopped when they saw us and then, funny it was, they smiled at us and started whacking the woman again, a girl really. I was angry but calm and I cocked my [rifle], flicked off the safety and pointed it straight at the bigger of the two and just said, "If you hit her again, my friend, I will f*cking shoot you right here and now." They stopped and ran away down the street, stopping only at the end to give us the two-fingered salute and then they disappeared. I'm thinking, "Is this why I joined the Army?"'

Mike Heavens, who served there with the 1st Battalion of the Glosters, recalls being sent alone by boat and train from Exeter to Londonderry, clutching two rifles and five rounds of ammunition along with all his other kit. 'At this time our task was to reassure the Catholic population that we would defend them from further violence from their Protestant neighbours and the locals were very pleasant and tea and biscuit stops were frequent and looked forward to. One or two of the guys played football for the local teams, one for the Bogside and another for the Creggan […] During our border patrols we spent a lot of time up at the BBC transmitter station in the hills above Derry, using a small caravan as a guard post, and on occasions we even nipped down to the village of Muff across in the south, in full fighting order, to attend the local dance there, leaving a guy outside to watch the vehicles as it didn't seem to matter much! The friendliness of the local Catholic population impressed us all and they really seemed to want us there. Christmas morning 1969 I was awakened by a gentle shaking and a young schoolgirl in her blue school uniform said in her lovely sing-song accent, "Merry Christmas soldier, and I hope you go home to your family in safety" and I was given a present, wrapped in Christmas paper, of a pair of socks, one of the nicest Christmas presents I have ever received. Then the girls sang a carol for us, whilst some very embarrassed squaddies looked on in awe. I never forgot the trusting and genuine smile of those schoolgirls and often wondered what happened to them and where did we go wrong to lose all that warmth and trust? Would I have got from Exeter to Londonderry just one year later? Certainly not like that trip!'

The change came in July 1970 with a three-day military clamp-down in the Falls area of West Belfast. From then on, journalist Fintan O'Toole says that, to the local population, 'both militarily and ideologically, the army was a player, not a referee'. The gloves were off.

As attacks increased, Dave, a veteran of the Royal Armoured Corps, remembers the arrival of two large boxes marked Made in the USA. 'These boxes contained our "flak jackets", all second-hand and very grubby with such legends as "Smoke Pot" and "Make Peace, Not War" written on them in biro. We found out that they had come from Vietnam. A few had bullet holes already in them and big brown stains which we knew to be old blood. They must have dragged them off soldiers' bodies to send them to us. "Charming", we thought.'

For Ken Wharton, the first impression of a tour in Northern Ireland was of 'how much Belfast was like the slums of my home town Leeds where I was brought up'. It was a common experience. Belfast and the towns and cities of Northern Ireland were, after all, part of the UK. The experience of conducting armed patrols along British streets was difficult. All around, men, women and children went about their daily lives seemingly oblivious to the soldiers crouching on street corners. Ernie Taylor of the Green Howards was reminded of this one day in 1972 when a car bomb exploded in Belfast.

I was watching the street when I heard a round go off. I cocked my [rifle] and I saw a man with what appeared to be a gun in his hand. I brought my rifle up into the aim position, got him in my sights and squeezed the trigger; nothing happened; misfire. I squeezed again and nothing; there's a guy in front of me with a weapon and I can't shoot him. Then, thank God, I looked again and the 'gunman' is a worker putting up some wooden boards with a nail gun after some IRA bomb damage. The sodding noise all sounds the same; what a lucky lad he was and I was even luckier as I wouldn't have wanted to live with that on my conscience. So many emotions went through my mind: what if I had killed an innocent man? What if he had been a gunman and I was sitting there, staring at the business end of his weapon and mine was useless?

Serving in Northern Ireland was no ordinary war. If soldiers came under attack, they knew that to fire back would make them criminally responsible for any civilian deaths. Lieutenant Tim G admitted that as a soldier it was difficult. 'Unfortunately I can only react, I can't initiate. Even in the dark we stand out like sore thumbs in our uniform. The terrorist can and does wear civilian clothes, coats with collars turned up, anoraks, and in his appearance there's nothing different about him to the ordinary civilian.'

The 'players', though, were known. Corporal Dick N, interviewed during a tour in Ireland in the 1980s, explained: 'It gives you a scary feeling if you're patrolling the streets when a man passes you who you know's involved with the terrorists. Your officers might not know him that well; or they might be letting him walk around so they can keep an eye on him and see where he goes. I didn't like it when someone did what they did to me last week. He said "Hello Dick" to me, just to let me know he knew my name and who I was.'

A former rifleman of the Royal Green Jackets complained that there was 'a lot of criticism in the papers about our shoot to kill policy. We talked about this a lot amongst ourselves and we were confused, because we were in a life and death situation and when we shot, we shot to stop the man with a gun or a man with a nail bomb. Of course we shot to kill; we aimed at the biggest target – the geezer's chest – just as we had been trained to do. A woman said to me when I was home on leave, "Why don't you shoot at their legs and wound them?" I said, "Mrs, this ain't

Hollywood, it's not a film and it's us or them." I was expecting her to advise us to shoot their weapons out of their hands! I mean how many POWs did the IRA take? I'll tell you something else: once we shot this geezer, our medic tried like hell to save his life, pumping his chest and trying to make him breathe. I couldn't see the IRA doing that!'

For the most part, soldiers rarely fired their weapons, unable to identify a clear target in the crowded streets where snipers waited. Instead, they were usually called upon to secure an area and pick up the pieces after another night of what started to be called 'an acceptable level of violence'. Airtrooper Scott Buchannan of the Army Air Corps was in Ireland towards the end of Operation Banner, when such events were commonplace.

One morning, very early, we were ordered out to a lonely country lane, just a few yards inside the Ulster border, as a body had been spotted, obviously dumped. It turned out to be the body of a female member of the IRA who had been 'turned' by our [Intelligence] boys but [the IRA] had discovered this and then tortured and killed her before tossing the body on the side of the road. They made a practice of booby-trapping bodies and it was not unusual to find a primed grenade or trembler device under the poor sod's body. They also had a habit of burying explosives in a ditch nearby and detonating them from their side of the border by remote control once the investigation team were on the spot.

This poor lady lay there for two days before the [bomb disposal] boys deemed it safe to remove her body. What a mess; the bastards had cut off both her breasts and dumped them next to her, she had been tortured with lit cigarette ends and worst of all, her body was burnt raw by a hot steam iron. Unmistakable shapes of the iron had been burned into her back in quite a few places. They did this as a warning to others not to inform on them. You couldn't call them animals as even animals don't behave in this way. I never did find out her name and her body was taken quietly away.

Operation Banner quickly settled down to a long, drawn-out battle of wills. Bombs struck the UK mainland and servicemen were ordered never to travel in uniform. Any soldier, anywhere, was a target. Typical of the attacks against the military was one carried out on 15 June 1988 in the town of Lisburn. Six soldiers, Ian Metcalfe (37), Michael Winkler (31), William Patterson (22), Mark Clavey (24) and Graham Lambie (22), all from the Royal Corps of Signals, and Derek Green (24) of the Royal Army Ordnance Corps, had been on a 'fun run' in the garrison town in order to raise funds for a local charity and were aboard a minibus taking them back to base when an IRA bomb planted underneath their vehicle exploded. In what many view as an alarming lapse of security, the six men were allowed to board the vehicle after it had been left unattended during the run. Many have felt that since Lisburn was such a major garrison town, full of military personnel, attacks were highly unlikely. Claims from the IRA that the device – at 7lbs, bigger than was the norm – had been designed to explode upwards in order to minimise civilian casualties, were discounted. The remark attracted derision in army and government circles. Had the area been packed with civilians, scores of others might have been killed or injured but, as American journalist P.J. O'Rourke found during a drinking session in a Republican bar, there were many who would consider it be an honour to be killed in an IRA attack. It was an attitude British soldiers found hard to understand.

Belfast social worker Marion Gibson recalls as 'one of the saddest moments of my professional life' an interview with a mother and her ten-year-old son. The boy had been trying to throw a petrol bomb at a passing army patrol but it had exploded and caused horrendous burns to his hand and arm. As they discussed the long series of operations and rehabilitation that would be needed, 'the mother said, "Isn't he a wee hero to the cause?" His scars were being viewed as marks of glory. It was hard to counsel in such a situation where "the cause" was seen worthy of such mutilation of a child.'

Hit and run attacks on vulnerable targets serve to erode the will of the soldier to fight. Together with the constant irritation of 'shit bombs' (crisp bags filled with excrement and thrown at foot patrols), taunts (more than one unit has been met by jeering crowds hopping and cheering after a soldier has lost a leg to a bomb) and a seemingly infinite variety of provocations, they are designed to provoke an overreaction by the troops. Any instance of the use of force, of retaliation, could be used by the propaganda machine to drum up more support. Any terrorist killed by the police or army with a weapon in his hands would become a martyr 'murdered by SAS assassins'. The army walked a fine line between being the soldiers they were and the policemen they had not trained to be.

Every day away from their normal duties reduced the efficiency of the tank crews and artillerymen assigned to the streets of Northern Ireland. Retraining could be costly so a routine developed of short 'Roulement' tours interspersed with service elsewhere. In 1982 the Royal Marines returned from the Falklands, took leave and then returned to Ireland. The routine was always the same, only the level of activity changed. For much of the 30 years of the army's presence, the experience was much the same.

Private Andy Bull of the Royal Regiment of Wales can never forget his first tour.

I was just 20 years of age when I was first posted to Northern Ireland with my battalion, the Royal Regiment of Wales, in November 1983. This tour was to be my first, having just missed out in 1981 where we were stationed in Aldershot, which was during the IRA hunger strikers' campaign. At that particular time I was only 17 years old and the requisite age for serving in Ulster was 18 years of age. We were to be stationed at McCrory Park police station in West Belfast, just off the Falls Road. The Falls Road, Springfield Road, Andersonstown and the Ballymurphy Estate were predominantly Roman Catholic and one of the hardcore heartlands of the IRA. We were transported from Aldergrove airport to West Belfast in 4-ton Bedford lorries, and it is fair to say that for the youngest there was lots of butterflies and adrenalin pumping. There was also an atmosphere of nervous anticipation for the expected and unexpected.

As you can imagine, our quarters were very cramped especially with all our equipment; mostly you were either lying on your bunk bed or sitting on it with a nice brew. When you were not on patrol you took advantage of a nice hot shower or the washrooms to do your laundry, or depending on what time you got back you would get your head down and catch up on some sleep. Sometimes sleep would prove very difficult because of the armoured PIGs [personnel carriers] which would be constantly roaring in and out of the fortified camp as well as the armoured Land Rovers. There was also the noise of the other boys snoring or farting and burping.

I can always remember my very first patrol, and the butterflies and adrenalin that were coursing through my body at that particular time. When you were in the briefing room and the intelligence officer was showing you photographs and video footage of the IRA players, it suddenly dawned on you that this was the real thing and that there was a great expectancy on you not to let your comrades down. I remember vividly our Corporal as he gave the order for us to load our magazines onto weapons but not to make ready. Seeing the high, heavy, reinforced camp double gates being pulled back and thinking to myself here we go, and the next moment I was sprinting and zig-zagging out into the streets of Belfast. I can remember the strange feeling of nakedness and awkwardness as I saw members of the public walking towards me for the very first time. Even though I was armed with an SLR rifle I could still feel my heart racing. I was like a coiled spring, not knowing if at any moment a sniper's rifle would ring out overhead or if a car would suddenly explode. As the patrol settled down into its role I slowly started to relax and to take in my surroundings and to run a critical eye over the painted tricolours and murals depicting IRA weapons on the walls and houses nearby. The civilian population paid us no heed during the day, but at night you were constantly verbally abused by drunks and gangs of youths looking for trouble.

As the days and weeks went by, you patrolled whether it rained, hailed or snowed. You found yourself becoming a part of Belfast, seeing the same people on a regular basis. We knew all the street names, knowing where all the different shops lay; a feeling as if you had been born or lived in Belfast all your life. However, you knew this was not true as the hard reality and brutal violence of the IRA would soon bloody the streets of Belfast once again. Sometimes on patrol we would escort the RUC and follow them into the pubs and clubs, especially if they were looking for a wanted IRA player. This was a dangerous time and the atmosphere of the pub would quickly change to hostility. We would take up our designated positions in the pub and take up a firing position to protect the policemen in the event of an incident. If hatred could be a living thing, you definitely saw it live and breathe in the eyes of those men in that pub that day. You knew from that moment on should you ever have the misfortune to fall into their hands, you would certainly be shown no mercy.

On 23 November 1983, just two months into our tour, whilst escorting two members of the RUC along a busy Falls Road, an IRA bomb exploded, severely injuring me and wounding my comrades and several civilians in the immediate vicinity. I was very fortunate that the Royal Victoria hospital was very nearby, and I know that had it not been for their medical and surgical skills that day I would not be writing this account today. The result of that terrorist bomb was to end my army career, and to rob me of something so precious and irreplaceable as my sight. It was to alter my life for ever, leaving me to begin a new challenge: that of entering civilian life as a blind man. I owe my life to the Royal Victoria hospital and to the doctors and nurses for saving my life that day.

Thirteen years later, little had changed. Andrew Thomas of the Royal Anglians arrived in Northern Ireland in November 1996. Already a veteran of Bosnia, he remembers his first patrol: 'I always remember to this day the sheer nerves and fright when we hard targeted out of the back gate from Springfield Road RUC station. We sprinted for about 50–80 yards zig-zagging. This was the worst time, exiting and entry to any RUC station or barracks.' He continues:

We then broke into a normal patrol pace. Pte Squibb was front man scout (he carried VJ [an electronic counter measure or ECM] to inform us of any bombs or devices anywhere). Lance Corporal Hedge was brick [a four man patrol unit] commander. I was third man. The task I had was to patrol backwards watching our brick's back. I carried the white sifter (ECM as well but a lot heavier) and also a baton gun. Fourth man was Private Killingsworth. He carried Antler, the heaviest of the ECM kit. We were covered by satellite teams on either side of us and a team in the rear giving us all-round defence.

Our patrol as I remember would take us into Falls Road and through the notorious RPG avenue [Beechmount Avenue], back through the Beechmounts and back into Springfield Road RUC station. It was a quick introduction by the Coldstream Guard Corporal and the Intelligence guy who were leaving Northern Ireland the same morning.

I remember heading onto the Falls Road and going firm in a firing position after carrying out 5- and 20-m metre checks [checking the area for any sign of any devices, bombs etc.]. We patrolled past a school for girls and I had never taken as much abuse as I took in that first 45-minute patrol. The shouts, the anger, the hatred and the sheer aggression in little girls' voices made me feel sad but also angry. Hard to believe a kid could be filled with so much hatred. We moved off and spotted a known IRA player, we stopped him and the RUC policeman searched and asked him some awkward questions. The player was let go and gave us a mouthful of abuse, something that would become familiar.

We went straight down the Falls Road and into RPG avenue. The sheer name could put the fright up many a good man! Then the stones, sticks, bottles and whatever else they could find flew in our direction. A huge house brick landed right on Pte Killingsworth's nose. Claret was all over the place. The kid ran off into the safety of all his mates and he was rewarded by a bag full of sweets for his efforts by a man also known as an IRA player! We managed to control the bleeding, and carried on with the patrol. Lance Corporal Hedge was keen not to let these bastards see Killer was hurt and carry on with the patrol.

We ran after the kids but soon learnt that it was not worth it. They soon disappeared into Belfast's back alleyways, and into friends' houses. We patrolled our way through the Beechmounts and back through Cavendish Street into Springfield Road RUC station. The things that amazed me on that first patrol were the hatred, the fear of talking to the British army, the spookiness of the place in general and the hiding places for easy guerrilla warfare for which the IRA was renowned.

For the young soldiers deployed on short tours, Northern Ireland could be a stressful place. The numbing boredom of endless patrols without any sign of terrorist activity could lead to potentially dangerous lapses of concentration, especially towards the end of the tour when minds were turning to thoughts of home. Lance Corporal 'Ossie' Osbourne of the Queen's Regiment was on patrol in the Turf Lodge area in 1989.

I went firm with my team outside a newsagents waiting to be called into the police station by the boss. My ex-partner had just given birth to my eldest son and I noticed a football in the shop window.

I am ashamed to admit it, but I started to daydream a little and imagined my son playing with the football at home in our garden. Suddenly I got the call over the radio to move into the RUC station and I instructed the lads to double in, which we did. As soon as we got in to the police station we were fastballed [deployed] back out to a street just a few yards from where I had gone firm just two minutes earlier. I held the team in their positions and waited for further instructions.

After about 30 minutes the lads and I were getting a little pissed off. We did not know why we were moved back out so quickly and had no idea how long we were going to have to stay out. I saw an RUC officer standing by the newsagent where I had been daydreaming just a short while earlier. I approached him and asked what was happening.

'You will not believe it,' he replied, 'this place has just been robbed and one of you lot were standing outside as it happened!'

'Oh really,' I said and slunk away feeling a little stupid!

It turned out that two lads had held up the newsagent with a pistol; they demanded all the fags and cash in the till. As the owner was about to start loading the swag into a bag I appeared in the window and scared the crap out of them. I had been too busy daydreaming and did not see a thing, even though I looked straight at them. Once I left, the two robbers fled with only 200 cigs to their name.

My chance of medals and fame was missed, all because of a football.

For the soldiers on short tours, Ireland was something to be endured, but each tour at least had a definite end. They knew when they would go home and that they simply had to stay alive until then. For their Irish colleagues, though, it could never be that simple. As one Ulster Defence Regiment soldier explained, 'We lived in the community we worked in –

we shopped, raised our kids, ate out, socialised, did everything that 'normal' life requires – but in the sight of our enemy. The same streets we lived on, we patrolled in uniform and did all the things the [Regular Army] did, but then had to go home at the end of the day and live a life.' Knowing they were vulnerable to attack at any time, even something as simple as the drive to and from work was fraught with risk.

Most of us commuted to and from work; some by rail, most by car, but I used to drive back and forth to work here – for a while I was part-time UDR – starting at 1930hrs and finishing at 0400hrs. I had a 20-mile drive through some 'areas of interest'.

'See you again lads.' With this cheery if tired farewell, I would go through the usual routine; beret, INIBA [body armour], webbing and combat jacket all would go into the boot. Cover with a blanket. Take out baggy boiler suit and squeeze it over your uniform. Gloves on – smaller size, fit like pilot's gloves. Save your hands getting cut to ribbons if the windscreen comes in. Start up, seat belt on – not law yet, but might save your life if something happens.

OK, here we go; out the gate, give the sentry the fingers, speed bumps, top of the road, no slowing, fast as she can take it, anyone could be waiting. Left? No, straight on, don't set a pattern; through the lights; red or not: stop for no man. Over the bridge, through the 'ville', keep going, no stopping, go, go out into the country. Past the County Hall, floor it down the long straight; did a VCP [vehicle check point] here just a couple of hours ago. Through the 'hog hill' – a type of chicane in the middle of the village – and then change down and speed through the diamond. Real country now, no street lights, eyes get used slowly to the dark; now there are bumpy culverts, rutted, shadowy, too fast to dwell on them.

Down the long hill, try not to slow for the corner at the bottom and then fly down the long sloped straight; tight corner and then down to third; look around for following lights; picked anyone up?

Big wall on the left, roadside monastery, tight left at the top; careful now. Past the cop shop, yellow sodium lights; did a LURK [observation of suspected terrorist location] on a house near here last week. Change down and then left into the Glenone; wide market street, deserted; no cars, over the bridge and into 'their' patch. Now my antenna switches on and past the pub at the crossroads; the villages from here are in 'enemy' territory. Good men have died in them. Through the village – VCP earlier too – down the hill, into the dark again with narrow roads, tension notches up a tad, past the corner, high hedges and then down to second for the last one, wait, wait for it, and then out into the open road, back up the gears, long straight, check the mirrors for lights. None; up to 75, 80, foot off gas for S-bends, crossroads; mirror again; bad roads here, culverts again, close to their area again.

Stretch of concrete road, it dips into dead ground with blind corners, over the crest and 'F*ck!' Jam on brakes, fishtail to a stop, just short of a car on its roof, heart going nineteen to the dozen; there's room to pass. Sneak a look into the car; no one in it, caused by some young lad with slower reactions than you. Phew! Up the hill and then floor it past the T-junction, then left, no slowing, past bingo hall, over the crossroads and as fast as possible into the dark again. Now it's the fun part; road narrows and as it dips, turn off the headlights: that should confuse the bastards. If they are waiting, they'll still hear me but won't see me straight off; buy some time. Then I'm through and nearly home.

Houses in a clump to the left; a few street lights cast a weak light; sharp left and then pull up at the door. I switch off the engine and listen to the silence then get out and listen again and enjoy the cooling wind. I find the keys, open the door – quietly, noisy git – boots off, sweating in the boiler suit. Sit in the chair and she finds you still there, three hours later.

Of the 197 UDR who were killed, the vast majority were killed in their own homes, in their own driveways, out shopping, at their civilian place of work, in front of their families, alone on country roads. And it didn't stop there – 57 ex-UDR members were killed in addition, some as long as ten years after leaving. Try to imagine living with that, not just for four months [the standard army tour of duty] but for the rest of your life. Even now we will never switch off. The awareness will never leave us. It has been part of our lives for too long.

Even before Operation Banner drew to an end, though, soldiers found themselves deployed to another civil war.

SOLDIER BY HARVEY ANDREWS

In a station in the city a British soldier stood
Talking to the people there if the people would
Some just stared in hatred, and others turned in pain
And the lonely British soldier wished he was back home again.

Come join the British Army! said the posters in his town
See the world and have your fun, come serve before the Crown.
The jobs were hard to come by and he could not face the dole
So he took his country's shilling and enlisted on the roll.

For there was no fear of fighting, the Empire long was lost
Just ten years in the army getting paid for being bossed.
Then leave a man experienced, a man who's made the grade.
A medal and a pension some mem'ries and a trade.

Then came the call for Ireland as the call had come before,
Another bloody chapter in an endless civil war.
The priests they stood on both sides, the priests they stood behind.
Another fight in Jesus' name, the blind against the blind,

The soldier stood between them between the whistling stones
And then the broken bottles that led to broken bones.
The petrol bombs that burnt his hands, the nails that pierced his skin,
And wished that he had stayed at home surrounded by his kin.

The station filled with people, the soldier soon was bored,
But better in the station than where the people warred.
The room filled up with mothers with daughters and with sons
Who stared with itchy fingers at the soldier and his gun.

A yell of fear a screech of brakes the shattering of glass,
The window of the station broke to let the package pass.
A scream came from the mothers as they ran towards the door
Dragging their children crying from the bomb upon the floor.

The soldier stood and could not move his gun he could not use,
He knew the bomb had seconds and not minutes on the fuse,
He could not run and pick it up and throw it in the street,
There were far too many people there too many running feet

Take cover! yelled the soldier, Take cover for your lives.
And the Irishmen threw down their young and stood before their wives,
They turned towards the soldier their eyes alive with fear
For God's sake save our children or they'll end their short lives here!

The soldier moved towards the bomb his stomach like a stone,
Why was this his battle God why was he alone?
He lay down on the package and he murmured one farewell
To those at home in England, to those he loved so well.

He saw the sights of summer felt the wind upon his brow
The young girls in the city parks how precious were they now
The soaring of the swallow the beauty of the swan
The music of the turning world so soon would it be gone.

A muffled soft explosion and the room began to quake,
The soldier blown across the floor his blood a crimson lake.
There was no time to cry or shout there was no time to moan,
And they turned their children's faces from the blood and from the bones.

The crowd outside soon gathered and the ambulances came
To carry off the body of a pawn lost in the game.
And the crowd they clapped and cheered and they sang their rebel song,
One soldier less to interfere where he did not belong.

And will the children growing up learn at their mothers' knees
The story of the soldier who bought their liberty
Who used his youthful body as a means towards an end
Who gave his life to those who called him murderer not friend?

CHAPTER FIVE
THE COURAGE TO DO NOTHING
BALKANS 1992–2007

When British forces were deployed to Bosnia in 1992 as part of the United Nations Protection Force (UNPROFOR), the then Defence Secretary, Malcolm Rifkind, predicted that their presence would be required for 12 months. As it turned out, their role was to change dramatically as the civil war in Bosnia became progressively more dangerous and unpredictable. Operation Grapple, as it was known, evolved into Operation Oculus and it would be 15 years before the last 630 British troops serving in Bosnia would be pulled out.

The 1st Battalion, the Cheshire Regiment battle group under Colonel 'Bosnia Bob' Stewart were sent to Bosnia in October 1992 and later strengthened by soldiers from the 2nd Battalion, Royal Irish Regiment, a squadron of 9th/12th Lancers and other units. From escorting humanitarian aid convoys, the troops switched to peacekeeping and finally direct intervention when NATO took over and launched a bombing campaign to force the warring parties to the negotiating table in Dayton, Ohio, in 1995.

Andrew Thomas, of the Royal Anglian Regiment, arrived in May 1994:

I was deployed on 14 May 1994 as part of Op Grapple 4 with my unit, the 2nd Battalion, the Royal Anglian Regiment known as the 'Poachers'. We were a mechanised unit based in Celle, Germany, part of 7th Armoured Brigade – the Desert Rats. We had received pre-Bosnia training in April prior to deployment, and were now operationally effective. I recall flying from Hanover airport into Split [on the Adriatic coast] where we were greeted by loud shouts and cheering [but] not for us, as we were here to relieve the Coldstream Guards. I and many others expected a war zone as soon as we touched down. However, we were met off the plane by beautiful Croatian air hostesses!

This was soon to change. After a meal and being rushed onto [trucks] all decked in UN white, we began our journey into Bosnia and the war zone we all expected. I felt nervous but yet [a kind of] looking forward sense of emotion. A sick feeling then hit my knotted guts, as we noticed building after building wrecked, burnt out and a cross placed on it! The Croats used this to identify where they had burnt a Muslim or Serb family out of their houses. We hit Mostar, where just days previously a section of about ten Malaysian UN soldiers had been killed by Serbs in the town.

As we debus from the vehicle, I always remember a slogan daubed on the walls. It said 'Welcome to Hell!' How correct that was to prove. We finally made to it Vitez school – it had been made a UN base as soon as the UN arrived [in the town] in 1993. After settling in for a few hours' sleep, I was warned that I would be out on the ground the following day and was to report at 0600hrs to Sgt Jim Matthews of the Mortar Platoon.

I woke up and was the only member of 8 platoon to be attached and on the ground so early. I met up with Sgt Matthews, there were eight of us on [Callsign] Bravo 8. It was a checkpoint, one side Croats and the other Muslim. Both these factions had declared a ceasefire the day before we had arrived in theatre. Yet the war [continued within] Serbian territory overlooking the town of Vitez and nearby Taffnik, where the checkpoint was located.

We had been checking vehicles and people to make sure they said who they were and where they where going. All seemed in order when early afternoon we started to hear what sounded like shells exploding not too far away. We knew this was incoming mortar rounds coming from the hills, where the Serbian stronghold was. We had no grounds to fire as we could not identify a target and under UN mandate we where not considered under threat.

The shelling was getting nearer. A nearby callsign patrolling came sprinting towards our [FV432 Armoured Personnel Carrier]. All four of the men took cover in our 432. I was on road duty but now battened down in the back along with ten others. The gunner reported he could not find any firing point.

A contact report was sent out by Sgt Keane [in command] of the patrol out on the ground. Two more rounds landed nearby and we heard an almighty crash. We knew this must have hit a house directly. The 432 was only equipped with a mounted 7-62 mm [machine gun]. We were all cramped and sweating tremendously, incoming rounds had stopped although we could still hear it in the distance. All of us were scared, but we hid it well!

Suddenly, as so often in Bosnia, it went quiet. It stayed that way for 30 minutes when the order from the ops room was to stand down and return to routine taskings. We dismounted out of the vehicle, stinking and sweaty but relieved to be out of there! We scanned and patrolled the area and noticed a house 50 metres away had been turned to rubble. We looked for casualties for a few hours but found nothing. The whole area and town remained that way all through the day and into the night. The scariest part was at night after the onslaught. I think that must be the scariest time I have experienced. Not the shelling, but the sheer silence. It really was hell in Bosnia.

As Major Roger Marshall of the Intelligence Corps later wrote, 'While wishing to be seen as having robust response capabilities, the UNPROFOR rules of engagement were not robust. The local joke was along the lines of "if you make a wrong move, I will speak to my colonel who will ask the general to ask our national defence minister to ask the prime minister to ask the rest of the UN to order me to open fire, so be warned."' As a result, UN soldiers were forced to sit by as all sides committed atrocities. Colonel Stewart gained a reputation for his willingness to use his troops to save lives. 'Lieutenant Colonel Stewart,' read his citation for the Distinguished Service Order awarded in 1993, 'has commanded the 1st Battalion The Cheshire Regiment Battalion Group for six months on an operational tour in Bosnia-Herzegovina under the auspices of the United Nations. He has been involved in Operation Grapple since the very beginning, and to him fell the responsibility for all the planning for the creation of a battalion base and a number of company bases in a region already in the throes of fierce inter-communal fighting. During this time, and throughout the tour, he has had to deal personally with a number of difficult local authorities. Throughout the tour, both he and his battalion, although neutral in their support of the delivery of aid by the United Nations High Commission for Refugees, have frequently been the target of attacks by one or other of the indigenous warring factions. Despite the limited mandate of the operation, Lieutenant Colonel Stewart chose, early on, to adopt a classic "hearts and minds" campaign to win the trust of those with whom he had to deal in order to ensure the free flow of aid. In doing so, he recognised that he was assuming a considerable personal risk, but his style of diplomacy and leadership and his determination to dominate paid handsome dividends and served as a marvellous example to the troops under his command. Throughout the tour, he has led right from the front, exercising all the energy, enthusiasm, charm and courage in his possession. On a number of occasions he has personally been the target of attack from either snipers, anti-tank fire or from mortar bombardment. On others, he was often caught in crossfire whilst conducting difficult and delicate negotiations but, on all occasions, he demonstrated cool and determined courage and inspirational leadership, never flinching from his duty [...] The outstanding success of the Battalion Group tour of duty owes an enormous amount to Lieutenant Colonel Stewart's unflagging energy, courage and leadership. He has sustained a high level of effort by the soldiers under his inspired command throughout a very difficult tour and under the most trying circumstances.'

Bosnia was a war unlike any the soldiers had encountered before. All sides argued that the UN, and Britain in particular, were siding with the enemy as aid was used as a weapon for the 'ethnic cleansing' of areas by denying supplies to one group or another. If supplies reached a group of refugees belonging to one faction, then the surrounding forces of the other factions would regard it as favouritism and use it to justify further attacks. The moral dilemma facing those sent on active service was encapsulated in a story by the correspondent Martin Bell, who hopes it is apocryphal, but suspects it isn't. 'It is about a journalist who wished to write a profile of a sniper on a front line in Sarajevo. The sniper was peering out from between two bricks in his forward defences. "What do you see?" asked the journalist.

"'I see two people walking in the street. Which of them do you want me to shoot?"

'It was at this point the journalist realized too late that he was in absolutely the wrong place at the wrong time, and engaged on a story that was fatally flawed and he should never have considered. He urged the sniper to shoot neither of them, fabricated some excuse and turned to leave.

'As he did so, he heard two shots of rapid fire from a position very close to him. "That was a pity," said the sniper. "You could have saved one of their lives."'

Scott Fraser, a veteran of the Gulf War, recalls Bosnia as the worst experience of his life.

The incident happened in January 1993 shortly after we deployed there as part of the UN Peacekeeping Force. One night we were evacuating civilians from a small town. It was like Armageddon. Fire, explosions, and constant gunfire. I saw a young girl, she was only four. I gave her a bar of chocolate from my ration pack. As she went to pick up the chocolate, she dropped her doll, and I bent down to pick it up. And that split second a sniper's bullet rang out and shot the little girl through the head. I have lived with that image in my head for years, and sometimes I wish that the bullet had hit me and spared the little girl's life. But, it wasn't to be.

There were, though, some successes for Fraser and his unit:

I remember one day, it was just after Christmas, and a convoy of medical supplies came to the HQ. We had to escort the convoy through the Serb Lines to a hospital full of very sick children. So, the convoy had to get through. My platoon was given this task. My commander had asked me before we set off to keep an eye on the new Platoon Commander. He had just joined us, and was a bit green. So we set off in our Warrior APCs [Armoured Personnel Carriers]. After about an hour, we came to this Serb checkpoint with land mines laid right across the road. We stopped and the Platoon Commander and our interpreter went across to the Serb Commander and asked him to remove the mines so that we could get by. The Serb refused to do so, my commander said that we were carrying medical supplies to a children's hospital and we had to get through. This did not make any difference, the Serb refused to budge. Throughout all this I'm sitting in the turret of my Warrior and watching, and I'm getting madder and madder.

So I put my pistol into my belt at my back and told my lads to cover me. I got out and went over to the Serb and I asked him to move the mines. Back came the same reply. I then asked the interpreter to tell the Serb to move them or I would attach one to his backside and throw him off the bridge. Still he wouldn't do it. Then I pulled out my pistol and pointed it at his head and said that I would count to ten and if he did not remove the mines I would blow his head off. I started to count out loud, 'one, two, three, four ...' He barked out an order and four of his men came out of this hut and removed the mines. Job Done. We got the convoy through the lines successfully to the hospital. Back at headquarters my Colonel asked me into his office and said to me, 'Would you have pulled that trigger?' I replied, 'That's one thing that you will never know Sir!' He replied, 'Well done, Jock.'

For the most part, the best the soldiers could do was to try to put themselves between the warring factions. A later report described how, 'Between April 1992 and March 1993, Srebrenica town and the villages in the area held by Bosnian Muslims were constantly subjected to Serb military assaults, including artillery attacks, sniper fire, and occasional bombing from aircraft. Each onslaught followed a similar pattern. Serb soldiers and paramilitaries surrounded a Bosnian Muslim village or hamlet, called upon the population to surrender their weapons, and then began with indiscriminate shelling and shooting. In most cases, they then entered the village or hamlet, expelled or killed the population, who offered no significant resistance, and destroyed their homes. During this period, Srebrenica was subjected to indiscriminate shelling from all directions on a daily basis. Potočari in particular was a daily target for Serb artillery and infantry because it was a sensitive point in the defence line around Srebrenica. Other Bosnian Muslim settlements were routinely attacked as well. All this resulted in a great number of refugees and casualties.'

Local Serb military and paramilitary forces from neighbouring parts of eastern Bosnia and Serbia gained control of Srebrenica for several weeks in early 1992, killing and expelling ethnic Bosniak civilians. In May 1992, Bosnian government forces recaptured the town and over the coming

97

year offensives by Bosnian forces increased the area under their control to a peak size of 900 square kilometres, although it remained, according to UN officials, 'a vulnerable island amid Serb-controlled territory'.

Over the next few months, the Serb military closed in around the town, forcing Bosniak residents of the outlying areas to flee to Srebrenica, whose population swelled to between 50,000 and 60,000 people. By the time Major Pyers Tucker of the Royal Regiment of Artillery arrived there as assistant to General Morillon, the French Commander of United Nations Forces in Bosnia-Herzegovina, the town was overcrowded and under siege. There was almost no running water, people relied on makeshift generators for electricity, while food, medicine and other essentials were extremely scarce. Before leaving, General Morillon told the panicked residents of Srebrenica at a public gathering that the town was under the protection of the UN and that he would never abandon them. Tucker, who worked an average of 17 hours a day, seven days a week during his tour as the General's aide, spent two weeks cut off in the town. Major Tucker, held hostage by the one factional group and constantly under fire from others, managed to send regular reports that kept the headquarters and the rest of the world informed of what was happening in the enclave. As Serb tanks and armoured personnel carriers advanced to cut off the aid convoy trying to reach the besieged town, Major Tucker parked his own armoured personnel carrier across the bridge and stood in front of the vehicle for two hours defying their advance. It was, as his later Military Cross citation put it, 'an act of conspicuous gallantry and probably saved the town that day'. Ultimately it was to prove fruitless. In 1995, as Serb forces closed in, the Dutch battalion stationed nearby closed its gates to the fleeing civilians and did nothing as women were raped and murdered in sight of armed UN troops. An unknown number of refugees were massacred and UN credibility crumbled.

On 12 March 1993, a joint British United Nations and United Nations Monitoring Organisation Group was sent to the town of Konjevic Polje in eastern Bosnia to evacuate wounded civilians and to rescue a World Health Organization doctor known to be working there. As they arrived and as Serb artillery fire intensified, the UN vehicles were mobbed by between two and three thousand terrified civilians demanding that the UN evacuate them. Lieutenant Nick Ilic, a native Croat speaker serving with the Light Infantry, tried to calm the situation but when the attack escalated with Serb tanks joining in the fire, a British military Foden recovery vehicle was hit and many of those around the convoy were either killed or injured. The situation was desperate and people in the crowd began to rock the British vehicles in a frenzy of fear. Lieutenant Ilic, together with a Russian United Nations military observer, decided that it was crucial to leave the safety of their armoured vehicle and try to calm the crowd. From then on, the two men remained outside their protective cover throughout the barrage, running backwards and forwards taking wounded civilians to shelter. As they worked to save the life of a wounded civilian, they found themselves faced by a hysterical local soldier who cocked his weapon and aimed it at them. Ilic managed to calm him down and returned to his task. According to his Queen's Gallantry Medal citation, 'Throughout 11th to 12th March Lieutenant Ilic was in considerable and constant danger, and often the risk to his own life was very great. He paid no heed to this and thought only of helping others. His reactions were outstanding and in the highest traditions of the Army.'

Nearby on the same operation, Warrant Officer Class II John McNair of the Royal Army Medical Corps had made contact with the World Health Organization doctor and began assisting with emergency operations on severely wounded civilians in the makeshift hospital or, more often, on the spot. Lacking any anaesthetic and even the most basic of surgical instruments, McNair was forced to perform several amputations using a pair of domestic scissors. When not assisting in surgical operations, McNair spent his time tending the injured. Several people, including some young children, died in his arms.

For most of those serving in Bosnia, the overwhelming feeling was one of frustration at the political and diplomatic shackles that prevented the soldiers from doing the job properly. Les Howard, serving with the Light Infantry, recalled being fired on at his base. Using rifle sights, he saw, 'about 75 metres away a man in combats firing a pistol at us. He seemed to be suffering from a stoppage after each shot as he kept cocking the weapon, but there was no mistaking where he was aiming. At that range he would be very lucky to hit us, so we stayed in cover and kept him under observation until he ran out of ammo and ran off. It might seem strange that we didn't return fire, but as the rounds were not falling all around us we were restricted under the UN rules of engagement and couldn't retaliate. I knew I could have dropped him with a single shot at that range, even in poor light, so he was lucky he was such a crap shot. Besides, I didn't want to spend the next week being interrogated by [the Military Police] and making endless statements if I had opened fire.'

Such random attacks were common, Howard says, as were problems with the various military and paramilitary groups that sprang up. The local police, for example, 'were always in pairs and were dressed in their new blue, black and white urban camouflage uniforms. They carried folding stock [Kalashnikov rifles] over their backs and wore pistol holsters on shiny leather belts. A few wore small black plastic hand grenades as well, but why a policeman needed one was beyond me. They would often saunter up to us, then after noticing the sentry they would brace up, pull the peaks of their baseball-style caps down over their eyes and act macho. One even put on a pair of sunglasses to beef up his act – at night! They thought they looked really hard, but to us they just looked like wannabe rappers on the way to a drive-by shooting. Wankers, but dangerous wankers!'

Witnessing the casual violence around them but being unable to do anything about it made Bosnia a difficult operational tour and it left many veterans scarred by what they had experienced. Hugh, a former Explosives Ordnance Disposal Operator who had served in the Gulf War, was in Bosnia in 1996 when he first started to find that experiences such as walking up to dead bodies were really playing on his mind. One day in Bosnia he witnessed a car crash and went to help the driver. While he was patching up the man's arm, 'the guy put a pistol to my head and said in broken English, "Eff off back to England. We don't want you here."' Then Hugh saw that the car was full of guns. He walked back to his vehicle, all the time 'expecting the back of my head and face to explode'.

Witnessing the effects of the war on children hurt most. Within hours of arriving in Pristina during the Kosovo operation, Private Peter Keegan, a Territorial Army medic, was called out to an area of waste ground where two children, a boy of nine and his 12-year-old sister, had stepped on a landmine. Her hair was curly, he recalled, his brown and in need of a trim. The mine had exploded between them, and each had one side of their body blown off, from head to foot. The curious thing was that the remaining half looked normal. The little girl was wearing jeans and a little summer top, the boy a T-shirt and trainers. 'It was a bizarre scene. I expected to see body parts scattered around, but there was nothing there.'

Beneath the company headquarters, a building formerly used by the Serbian police, Keegan and his fellow soldiers found a hidden torture chamber. 'There were shackles and chains on the walls, blood all over the floor and human heads stacked in a corner, half a dozen of them, all of young men. We found a sword and handed it over to the United Nations police.' It was only the start of his six-month tour.

In the late 1990s the Canadian media reported that their soldiers who acted as peacekeepers in Bosnia suffered from numerous attacks of anxiety and depression when they returned from the front. Author Wendy Holden, in her study *Shell Shock*, points out that peacekeepers suffer from the fact that they must observe atrocities but are helpless to fight back or to defend adequately those they have been sent to save. 'Proud to become professional soldiers and keen to fight a war, they are, however, distanced from death and the reality of killing. They are members of a society that finds fatalities unimaginable. When presented with the unimaginable, they crack.'

In May 2008 a service was held at the Armed Forces Memorial, Staffordshire, to give thanks to those members of the British Armed Forces who served in Bosnia and Herzegovina, and also to mark the withdrawal of UK troops from the country in 2007. Nick Ilic, by then promoted to Major, said:

> For those of us who deployed to Bosnia, in the autumn of 1992, we were confronted with a situation that few of us knew how to deal with. Our mission was to assist in the delivery of humanitarian aid to the people of Bosnia and Herzegovina. It was carried out in the most difficult of conditions, when war was in full swing. The result was that we all witnessed what was good and also evil about humanity. The fighting exposed us to sights that we never thought we would witness in Europe, and thought had been consigned to history.
>
> The suffering we witnessed made our resolve to succeed that much stronger – and we did succeed. There is no doubt that, by placing ourselves in the line of fire, we saved lives.
>
> However, it came at a cost in terms of lives. For this reason it is only right that the sacrifice made by the UK Armed Forces in Bosnia and Herzegovina is recognised by this commemorative event. For many, including myself, it will bring back difficult memories and emotions.

Over 60 British servicemen and women died during Operation Grapple from various causes. At least 12 more died in similar operations in Kosovo. During that time, soldiers were called upon to undertake peacekeeping duties in the Balkans and Northern Ireland but these were also interspersed with more offensive operations – 'real wars'.

CHAPTER SIX
FIX BAYONETS

The last order we heard was, 'Fix bayonets and die like British soldiers do.'

London newspaper the Graphic, reporting on Rorke's Drift in
the Anglo-Zulu War, 1879

We like to think of ourselves as a peaceful nation, and so our wars tend to start with a retreat and a last-ditch defence to buy time to rally the small, ill-equipped army we have available. The opening retreat, be it to Corunna, from Kabul, from Mons or to Dunkirk, has been a common feature of Britain's wars. In 1918, as the great German offensive smashed through the Allied lines, thousands of men stood and fought to the death to buy time for others behind them to halt the retreat, regroup and turn the tide. Twenty-two years later, their sons fought and died on the same killing fields and for much the same reason.

In May 1940 the British Expeditionary Force in France had been wrong-footed by the Germans, with all the frontline units having moved north into Belgium to meet one invading force. Then, another, larger

Panzer army crashed through northern France where the only troops available to stop them were from the Territorial Army, sent to France solely to act as a labour force and who were, as one CO later described them, 'untrained and virtually unarmed'. As one group tried to stop a German tank column, they found the few anti-tank weapons they had been issued had come with training ammunition – they were merely, in the eyes of many, an untrained unit with no need of the real thing. The pitiful artillery support on offer made the Germans think they had interrupted a training exercise. Why else would the artillery limbers be filled with blank ammunition?

Just after 0900hrs on 20 May, Colonel Swinburne of the newly reformed Tyneside Scottish was tasked with holding a section of the line. He ordered Second Lieutenant Stordy to take two sections by truck to secure the right flank at the junction of the road to Ficheux. Taking a Bren light machine gun and a Boys anti-tank rifle, Stordy set out in the lead truck and took up position around the home of the Cagin family at the junction of the Bucquoy and Ficheux roads. At the same time, Lieutenant MacGregor was tasked with a reconnaissance towards Saulty from where he made contact with the left company of the Buffs, who had also been ordered forward.

With everything apparently going to plan, Swinburne then set out in an 8cwt truck, escorted by Second Lieutenant Cohen and three men, to establish contact with brigade HQ, just 3 kilometres away at Barly. Behind him, seven trucks carrying HQ Company and a mixed group of store men and labourers hurriedly attached to make up the numbers, followed along the road towards Ficheux. At about 0915hrs, as the trucks drew near the Darras farm, machine guns of the 3rd Company, 8th Motorised Battalion of 8th Panzer Division opened up from their ambush.

Private Ross, in one of the trucks behind Swinburne, recalled: 'We'd only travelled a short distance when we came under heavy machine gun fire. Our driver was killed and the lorry left the road after it had just passed in front of a farm, where there was a stable. One of our vehicles was on fire. Another with the water tank headed towards the fields. The enemy fire was coming from the south west […] CSM Swordy, our oldest NCO, set up some defensive positions [but] we only had rifles and a single anti-tank weapon. As we had some casualties leaving the lorry, I received the order to set up a first aid post. I went behind the stable when, all of a sudden, a fire broke out. There were a number of pigs with their skin on fire who were running in all directions. I then decided to take the wounded to the other side of the road towards a cattle trough. Piper Eadie and myself improvised a stretcher and carried those who couldn't walk to this new position.'

Nearby, Private Malcolm Armstrong had also been in the convoy: 'In my vehicle [39-year-old Private Arthur] Todhunter had been shot in the head. I was at the rear of the vehicle crouching down and shouting to him to get out which he couldn't do as he was already dead. There was panic everywhere. I went round to the left and saw a small tank approaching. We were given the order to fix bayonets to attack. Surprised, I noticed that the cannon turned towards me but I escaped death when he changed direction, fired and one of the other lads fell. With Private Albert Foster, who was killed later, we advanced along the side of the Pronier Farm. I was going to go in when a bullet or something similar struck my rifle and I dropped it. As I bent down to pick it up I was again saved when something just missed me. I then ran to an area behind this building and saw a dozen of my comrades mown down by machine gun fire. I quickly lay down behind them and was wounded by mortar fire. I put on a field dressing and, as there were Germans everywhere, I surrendered.'

The opening fusillade had hit the windscreen and engine of Swinburne's vehicle and set it on fire. Cut off from his battalion, he began making his way forward in the hope of reaching Brigade HQ, but found himself surrounded. He was eventually captured two nights later in the village of Avesnes-les-Comtes.

Behind him, his battalion was in chaos. German infantry, tanks and armoured cars were closing in from all sides. In open ground, without cover or heavy weapons, the Tyneside Scottish stood little chance. The battle quickly deteriorated into a series of individual engagements. Company Sergeant Major Baggs later recalled that within minutes he had 14 killed and 6 wounded as he and his men were caught in the open by enfilade fire. After struggling into the scant cover of the railway embankment, the Germans were able to bring up two tanks and blasted them out of their position. With no other option, Baggs surrendered.

Elsewhere, the Tynesiders were determined to go down fighting. At the Pronier Farm, Provost Sergeant Dick Chambers was seen to charge an enemy tank and was killed as he tried to fire through the slits in the turret. Company Sergeant Major Newton calmly strolled around his men's positions describing how 'interesting' the situation had become and how he had been wounded in this same area in the First War. Company Sergeant Majors Morris and Parmenter both took over Boys rifles whose crews had been killed and kept up what fire they could until they, too, were overrun. Lance Corporal Laidler carried with him regimental bagpipes that had been used in action at La Boiselle on 1 July 1916 when the pipers had led the attack, only to be gunned down. Now, Laidler played again. A junior NCO, only recently promoted, was heard giving textbook fire direction commands for targets just yards away – completely unnecessary but with the great effect of maintaining discipline while two new recruits, wounded manning a roadblock, refused to accept treatment and remained at their posts until overrun.

As fighting continued through the morning, exhausted men were seen to fall asleep even under fire. It was a one-sided battle, all the more so when a number of the Lewis guns that had been hurriedly issued to them were found to be marked 'DP' – for drill purposes only and incapable of firing a shot. Despite these handicaps, though, the teenagers of Recruit Company were determined to prove themselves. In a day of doomed courage, theirs was a story that epitomised the plight facing the beleaguered labour divisions. 'Their ammunition expended,' the Tynesiders' history records, 'a section of recruits with under eight weeks' training calmly obeyed the order to fix bayonets and meet the attack of an enemy AFV [armoured fighting vehicle] that was approaching them – a futile but heroic gesture. Surrender never occurred to them'. In all, four Military Crosses, one Distinguished Conduct Medal, four Military Medals and twenty Mentions in Dispatches were won, but they came at a high price. Reports vary, but estimates suggest that no more than 80 of the battalion's 750 men escaped death or capture and that most of those captured surrendered only after being wounded.

To the south, men of the Royal Sussex fired a mortar barrage of smoke shells – the only ammunition they had – and they, too, fixed bayonets and charged the German tanks. All along the line, men with only a few weeks' training and equipped with only the most basic weapons, fought to the death because they had been told that they had to buy time for the BEF to reorganise. In years to come, for the French, the events of 1940 more than confirmed their belief that 'perfidious Albion' had deserted them in their time of need. Yet for the villagers of La Herlière that never seemed true. The speed of the German advance had caught many civilians before they could flee, so the people of the area knew about Private John Lungley, a 34-year-old Bren gunner of the 5th Buffs. On 20 May he was left alone in a slit trench as the Germans closed in. They broke off their attack and called on him to surrender. He refused. They attacked again. Again he held them back. A tank was called up and he died at his post. That night, and every night, flowers appeared on his temporary grave. When it was decided to take his body to the local cemetery, so many locals turned out to honour him that the angry Germans cancelled the ceremony and buried him at night. No one at La Herlière believed the British had deserted them.

A German account of the battle for France records the comments of a Sergeant in 'the Yorkshire Regiment' taken prisoner at Dunkirk. 'My regiment has suffered great losses, every tenth man has been killed. The German artillery is very good, the German infantrist [sic] fights very courageously. Yes, we have great respect for you. We knew that your

Division had fought in Poland, and has been called since "the bloody dogs". That is true. But we will beat you next time all the same.' A report produced by the German IV Corps described the British troops they encountered as men who 'did not complain of hardships. In battle [they were] tough and dogged [...] In defence the Englishman took any punishment that came his way.'

In the months following the fall of France, Britain prepared itself for invasion. Across the country, many thousands of men who were too old or too young for military service volunteered for the Home Guard. They knew they faced a powerful German military, armed in some cases with little more than bags of pepper. 'We thought we'd be able to hold them up for about an hour,' one veteran explained. 'It'd take them about fifty minutes to stop laughing and then they'd roll straight over us.' Bumbling amateurs of *Dad's Army* they may have been, but the thought of not fighting to defend their homes never occurred to them. A select few were specially trained to go underground and to fight as a resistance army behind enemy lines; their hidden bunkers still dot the landscape today. They were told their life expectancy would be a matter of weeks at best and that to survive even that long would entail the assassination of key local figures – their friends, their neighbours, even their own families – to prevent their discovery. They lived with the knowledge that the people they spoke to every day might soon be a target.

Ten years later, British troops faced another enemy. On 25 June 1950, the South Korean army was organised only for defence. It had some eight divisions scattered along the frontier with the north but no heavy artillery or air support. When the North Korean army invaded it had artillery and mortars, about 100 Soviet-built tanks and an efficient, modern air force. The South Koreans were unable to put up any prolonged resistance and in just five days the capital, Seoul, was in the hands of the enemy and the forces of the Republic were in full retreat to the south. The nearest American forces were in Japan and consisted of only two weak divisions on garrison duty. They were rushed forward and thrown piecemeal into the battle to try and stem the speed of the invasion. By the middle of August they were fighting desperately to hold the slowly shrinking bridgehead round Pusan so that the reinforcements being hurried from America would be able to land.

A small British contingent was requested as part of a UN operation, and on 25 August men of the Middlesex Regiment with Brigade Headquarters in the light aircraft carrier HMS *Unicorn*, and the Argyll and Sutherland Highlanders in the cruiser HMS *Ceylon*, left Hong Kong. As they departed, General Sir John Harding, the Commander-in-Chief of the Far East Land Forces, visited them. As one history of the campaign recalls, he 'exhorted them to maintain that great British military tradition of standing your ground when ordered to do so, he advised them not to worry if snipers slipped round their flank or guerrillas attacked them from the rear, and he told them that the honour of the British Army and British people rested in their hands. He finished by reading out a message from General MacArthur, expressing his thanks and appreciation at the news of British reinforcements. General MacArthur's message ended in these words: "They will add new lustre to British arms. They will have a warm welcome when they arrive here, and will receive my personal attention."'

The ships docked at noon on 29 August with the pipes and drums playing from the top of the rear gun turret and to a great welcome – an American band, a Korean band and a large party of schoolchildren singing 'God Save the King'. As he left the ship at the head of his men, Major Kenneth Muir was presented with a bouquet by two Korean children but, despite the ceremony, there was a real sense of urgency. The position at the front was known to be critical as exhausted American troops tried desperately to defend the perimeter of the bridgehead, and it was soon clear that the Brigade was needed for immediate action, even before the arrival of its vehicles and heavy equipment.

On 5 September the British force took over responsibility for a section of the Allied line about 11,000 yards long on the Naktong River south west of Taegu. Within 11 days of leaving Hong Kong they were in position and in sight of the enemy.

'There is no doubt that all ranks of the Middlesex and Argylls were fully conscious of the fact that they were representing the British Army,' comments the official history, 'and that the eyes of not only the American Command but of the whole world were upon them. It was in this spirit that they started the campaign, and it never flagged – indeed, it was passed on to their successors, and it was just that spirit that animated later the Commonwealth Division and made it the fine fighting machine it turned out to be.'

By mid-September the build-up of the United Nations Forces had reached the point where it seemed possible to go on the attack to regain some of the ground lost to the North Koreans. Plans had already been made to break out of the bridgehead, cross the Naktong River and drive the enemy westwards and northwards in conjunction with the landing of other American forces at Inchon. On the night of 22 September the 1st Battalion, Argyll and Sutherland Highlanders moved across the river to support the left flank of the breakout attempt and lead an assault to capture Hill 282.

By nightfall on the following day they were at the base of Hill 282 and began to dig in. The Americans had promised artillery for the next day's attack so the Argylls attempted to get some sleep, while more ammunition and food were brought up to them. At 4am the attack company was roused and started up the hill tracks but as the sky lightened, enemy automatic weapons and mortars opened up. Ex-Argyll Pat Quinn remembers the battle: 'We were told that the attack was to be a surprise with no artillery softening up or pre-aerial bombardment to give the enemy a rude awaking. B Company was chosen to lead the assault with C Company hard on their heels. The hill was steep and covered with scrub, loose rocks and fir trees. The North Koreans were not used to being attacked at 5am and the leading Argylls were able to get within 50 yards before making their charge. Recovering quickly from the initial shock, the

North Koreans opened up with everything they had and killed the leading platoon commanders among others. It was at this stage that we went into a classic copybook Highlander charge, yelling like banshees and using our rifles and bayonets to clear the North Korean positions. It was too much for the North Koreans and those who were left alive left the scene. We had taken Hill 282.'

'Some difficulty was experienced in evacuating the wounded from the position and demands were made for stretcher-bearing parties to be sent forward by the Battalion,' reads Major Muir's citation. Muir was at the Battalion HQ on nearby Point 148 when the request came in and immediately suggested that he take command of a group of 30 men who were being readied to evacuate the casualties. The Brigade Commander agreed. The citation continues:

At approximately 0900 hrs a stretcher-bearing party arrived and with it came the Battalion Second-in-Command, Major K. Muir. He proceeded to organise the evacuation of the casualties. At approximately 0930 hours, small parties of the enemy started to infiltrate on the left flank necessitating the reinforcing of the forward platoon. For the next hour this infiltration increased, as did the shelling and mortaring, causing further casualties within the two companies. By 1100 hours, casualties were moderately severe and some difficulty was being experienced in holding the enemy. In addition, due to reinforcing the left flank and providing personnel to assist with the wounded, both companies were so inextricably mixed that it was obvious that they must come under a unified command. Major Muir, although only visiting the position, automatically took over command and with complete disregard for his own personal safety, started to move around the forward elements, cheering on and encouraging the men to greater efforts despite the fact that ammunition was running low. He was continually under enemy fire, and, despite entreaties from officers and men alike, refused to take cover.

'There was no rest for us [after taking the hill],' says Quinn. 'Hill 388 on which the North Koreans were well positioned overlooked Hill 282 from the side of the saddle. They started to shell us and we were soon pinned down. Urgent calls were made for artillery support, but there was none to be had. Some nameless Napoleon far behind the lines had ordered the gunners elsewhere and left us high and dry with no fire support [...] Major Muir asked for an air strike on the North Korean reserves that could be seen moving up to the left of our position. After getting confirmation that an air strike was on its way, the Major made sure that our positions were clearly marked from the air by using crimson and yellow recognition panels.

'Shortly after 12 noon three American P-51 Mustang aircraft appeared. We all cheered at the sight of these aircraft, feeling that the odds were now in our favour. Our cheers soon turned to horror as the American aircraft ignored our recognition panels and swept down on our positions with all guns blazing, killing many Argylls. The aircraft then circled once and came back in for another run. This time they dropped deadly napalm bombs on us.'

In just two minutes the so-called 'friendly fire' from the planes had virtually wiped out B Company. Seventeen soldiers died instantly in the attack. But 76 others suffered horrifying burns in the inferno. Geordie Shearer was 19 years old at the time and remembers trying to help his friend Davie Simpson: 'He was just lying there covered in burns so I gave him a cigarette. He took a puff and when I tried to take the cigarette from his mouth, his lip came away with it.' Simpson survived his injuries and remembers: 'We set off early in the morning and took the hill in record time. When we got to the top we put out our air recognition panels. We were told to dig in but the hill was like concrete. The next thing I knew was that we were covered in flames. I rolled down the hill so far and then walked. The skin on my arms was hanging in sheets. I must have passed out because the next thing I remember is waking up on a stretcher in an American aid post.'

Douglas Haldane was the battalion's medical officer. 'A number of the Jocks who were still alive were very badly burned. We used intravenous plasma, which was very unusual for us. But the guys who perished were in a real mess. Eighty per cent of their bodies were covered in burns.' His Sergeant, Dougie Cooper, also remembers that terrible day. 'We were left to pick up the pieces. Napalm burns the skin. When the US planes used it on the North Koreans, we often heard them screaming to die.'

The attack forced the defenders off the hilltop and into positions about 50 feet below the crest. The dazed survivors struggled to gather their dead, dying and wounded as the North Koreans realised what had happened and charged the hill. One lone soldier, Private Watts, kept the attackers at a distance as a handful of soldiers regrouped and came to his aid. Major Muir, one of the survivors, decided that the charred and smouldering hilltop must be immediately reoccupied. Collecting about 35 Argylls, he led them back up the hill under heavy enemy fire. Pat Quinn was one of them: 'The Argylls were shot and barbecued and blasted off our hill. The 35 survivors of the American air strike rallied together and led by Major Muir we managed to reoccupy the still burning hill.'

Waves of North Koreans were by now attacking from three directions and threatening to cut off the small force entirely. Ammunition was running low and Major Gordon-Ingram with six other Argylls gave covering fire to 14 others gathering what they could from the dead and wounded, as Major Muir himself fired the company's sole remaining 2-inch mortar. The fighting was fierce and at close quarters. Twenty-three-year-old Private Eric Gurr didn't remember the sounds of the first burst of bullets that slammed through his legs, clipping one and hitting his thumb, but as he fell back and played dead all he could hear was the strains of enemy bugles. He fell and hid among the corpses around him, feeling a long way from home. Another round hit his shoulder and he passed out. He came around to find an enemy soldier searching his pockets. Sixty years later he says that not a day passes that he doesn't think of what happened next: 'He motioned to me to stay still and silent and to put my hands over my head and then he left me. I kept waiting for the bullet to come and kill me, but it never did. I went on to live another 60 years, to have a happy marriage and raise two great kids and a lot of guys didn't get that chance.' Gurr was one of only two survivors found on the hill when Australian troops retook it.

'Grossly outnumbered and under heavy automatic fire,' the official account goes on, 'Major Muir moved about his small force re-distributing fast-diminishing ammunition, and when the ammunition for his own weapon was spent, he took over a 2-inch mortar which he used with very great effect against the enemy. While firing the mortar, he was still shouting encouragement and advice to his men and for a further five minutes the enemy were held. Finally, Major Muir was hit with two bursts of automatic fire which mortally wounded him, but even then he retained consciousness and was still as determined to fight on. His last words were: "The G**ks will never drive the Argylls off this hill."'

'With all our ammunition all gone and scarcely a man still unwounded,' says Quinn, 'it was time to leave the hill. The battle-exhausted survivors came down the hill carrying or dragging the wounded. I was so badly wounded that I could not walk and had to be dragged down the hill, but at least I was still alive.'

At the bottom of the hill they were met by five American tanks from 24th Recon Company of the 24th Infantry Division, sent to give what support they could. Herman Hall, one of the tank crewmen involved, wrote later that '[we] had been in Korea since 4 July 1950. [Our] unit I would say was as good as any unit in Korea and had the terrain been different our tanks would have given support. All we could do was witness the events. I did see the panels and they were the right colour [...] I watched in horror as the three P-51 Mustangs strafed and napalmed the troops. That was one of the saddest days of my life and I know every man in my company on that day will never forget [it].' While he and his fellow tankers were 'dodging mortar shells and helping our wounded, the

Argylls were coming down the road, about 900 yards or so from Hill 282 and as the lead men were within 10 feet of where I was standing one of the men was hit and just as quickly a few others covered his body. I asked why they covered him and the reply was, "We cover our guys when they get hit. That way they have a better chance of surviving if only being hit once." That is when I realized these guys really had it! Until that time I was a little in doubt because just prior they were all singing the song "If I knew you were coming I would've baked a cake". Not forgotten, never.'

Major Kenneth Muir was 38 years old and the son of a previous battalion commander. He was awarded the Victoria Cross for his actions.

Wars, though, are not won by defensive actions. A US Army study published after War World II by Colonel S.L.A. Marshall looked into the effectiveness of US infantrymen in the period 1943–45 and found only 15 per cent of trained combat riflemen used their weapons in battle – the rest did not run away, but even under attack they would not kill. 'The thing is simply this,' wrote Marshall, 'that out of an average 100 men along the line of fire during the period of an encounter, only 15 men on average would take any part with the weapons. This was true whether the action was spread over a day, or two days or three [...] In the most aggressive infantry companies, under the most intense local pressure, the figure rarely rose above 25 per cent of total strength from the opening to the close of an action.'

Training of infantrymen changed as a result. The aim of the soldier today is what it's always been, but now the message from the outset is clear. The mission is to close with the enemy and to kill him. 'You don't win wars by dying for your country,' Patton told his troops, 'but by making the other fellow die for his.' Modern combat training is about teaching the recruit to fear letting his mates down more than anything else and to value controlled aggression, fostering the belief that the soldier's true aim was 'to provide the enemy with the maximum opportunity to die for his country'.

On the way to the South Atlantic, British journalists Patrick Bishop and John Witherow had observed training sessions with some disquiet. They described one in their book *The Winter War*: "'What do you do if you find a wounded Argie?' asked a Para corporal, rhetorically, to a platoon weapons talk. "You blow his f*cking head off. What do you do if there's a TV crew watching? You treat him as one of your own" [...] Many of the Toms, as the Para officers called their men with a mixture of affection and contempt, enjoyed their image as emotionless, efficient killers, one step away from being psychopaths [...] I asked one [...] what he would do if he found a wounded Argie. "Kill him with me bayonet, rip his gold teeth out and cut off his fingers to get his rings," he replied. Of course, they did nothing of the sort when the hypothesis became real. But they would like you to think they would.'

This spirit of aggression won through against the odds. Fear of what combat might be like disappeared as the battle skills that had been endlessly practised clicked in. Soldiers find themselves reacting immediately and instinctively to the situation with a strange mixture of excitement and terror. As S.A. Stouffer found among American troops in the Pacific theatre in 1944, a survey of 2,000 soldiers looked at how fear in action manifested itself. It showed that 84 per cent said they experienced a violent pounding of the heart, others felt sick. About half said they felt faint. A quarter said they had vomited and 21 per cent admitted to having lost control of their bowels. Since this figure is based on voluntary admissions, we could perhaps expect the true figures to be higher. On the battlefield, shit happens.

There is also exhilaration in the horror. 'The closest guy I ever killed,' said a former Special Forces soldier, 'was about 3 feet away from me. At that distance, they explode when you hit them with a burst [...] that's what's happening to the lads when they're doing house clearances – you're face to face. And it stays with you.' Being at the centre of a firefight, he said, 'was like a hard on. It's exciting. You do it because you believe in what you're doing right then and there.'

Dom Gray, a Falklands veteran of 3 Para's bayonet attack on Longdon, described it as 'a joy'. Major Robert Lawrence of the Scots Guards, who won the Military Cross on nearby Mount Tumbledown, recalls his experiences during the battle. 'I took off, and screamed at my men to follow me. In that instant, my one sudden thought was, are they going to follow me, or will I be left to run off on my own? But when I glanced round, there was this unbelievably fantastic sight of every man getting up and running in. I remember thinking at that moment that this was life on a knife-edge. Amazing. Fantastic. Nothing would ever bother me again from then on.' The adrenalin rush carried them forward into the Argentine positions. As dawn broke, Lawrence saw an Argentine lying in the rocks. 'I thought to myself, is he alive or dead? But instead of just kicking or prodding him, I stuck my bayonet into the back of his arm, dug it right in because I had run out of ammunition. He spun wildly on the ground, and my bayonet snapped. And as he spun, he was trying to get a Colt 45 out of an army holster on his waist. So I had to stab him to death. I stabbed him and I stabbed him, again and again, in the mouth, in the face, in the guts, with a snapped bayonet. It was absolutely horrific. Stabbing a man to death is not a clean way to kill somebody, and what made it doubly horrific was that at one point he started screaming "Please!" in English to me. But had I left him he could have ended up shooting me in the back.'

Pressing on, Lawrence led his men to the very summit of Tumbledown where the lights of Port Stanley could be seen below. 'I turned to Guardsman McEntaggart as we went along and, for some inexplicable reason, suddenly cried out "Isn't this fun?" He took a few last steps forward. Seconds later, a high velocity round travelling at 3,800 feet per second shattered Lawrence's skull.'

CHAPTER SEVEN

CASEVAC

The bodybags arrived in wrappers that stated: 'plastic bags can cause suffocation'.

Afghanistan veteran

Lawrence was casevaced (casualty evacuation) from the battlefield. 'I found out later,' he says, 'that the pilot of this Scout helicopter, Captain Sammy Drennan, shouldn't really have been there as he was over the line on his map that he had been told not to cross. Sammy had been a Scots Guards Colour Sergeant before transferring to the Army Air Corps, and apparently when he heard about the number of casualties his old regiment was suffering he decided he'd go in and get some out if he could. Had he been shot down in the process – for undoubtedly he was an Argentinean target – he might well have been reprimanded. As it was, he didn't get shot down and he was awarded a Distinguished Flying Cross.'

Sammy's was one of many awards that have been granted for saving, not taking lives. Often the most heroic are those who do not – will not – fight. There is an unwritten rule for all soldiers. Whatever happens, you know that if you are hurt, people will come for you. They will die for you. But they won't leave you. It comes as no surprise to veterans that in the entire history of the decoration, only three men have ever won the Victoria Cross twice. Two, Noel Godfrey Chavasse and Arthur Martin-Leake, were medics.

One of the most highly decorated of all soldiers of World War I, Lance Corporal Bill Coltman, was a pacifist stretcher-bearer. Born in 1891, Coltman was deeply religious and a lay preacher in the non-conformist Christian group, The Brethren. He volunteered at the outbreak of World War I and joined the 6th Battalion of the North Staffordshire Regiment as a rifleman but felt he could not take life. 'I don't believe in guns and war,' he said later. To him the idea of killing another human being was simply unimaginable. If he were to play any role at all, it would be to save lives, not take them. Instead, he volunteered as a stretcher-bearer to carry the wounded from the battlefield to the frontline aid posts.

It was in this role that the 5'4" Coltman, whom his grandchildren remember only as 'quiet and unassuming', came to win the Victoria Cross, two Distinguished Conduct Medals, two Military Medals and a Mention in Dispatches for returning time and again to use his own body to shield the injured as he brought them back from no man's land. His citations included a catalogue of courage and devotion to duty. The *London Gazette* of 26 March 1917 wrote: 'Near Monchy on 17 February 1917, during misty weather, an officer took out a party to repair the wire in front of the trenches. The mist suddenly cleared and the enemy opened fire. The officer sent the party in, and was himself the last to withdraw. When getting through our wire he was shot through the thigh and fell. Private Coltman, with conspicuous gallantry, in full view of the enemy, without hesitation went out from the trenches to this officer, and with difficulty succeeded in bringing him in through the wire, and while doing so he displayed great courage in keeping himself between his officer and the enemy, although being only 85 yards from the hostile trenches and under rifle fire the whole time. Private Coltman has previously shown great gallantry as a stretcher-bearer, particularly on 1 July 1916.'

It was followed on 16 August 1917 by an award for 'Several incidents: In the trenches near Lens, Lance Corporal (stretcher-bearer) Coltman has shown great gallantry, devotion to duty and disregard for personal danger on three occasions:

'6 June 1917. A mortar bomb set fire to the Company dump wherein bombs and rockets were stored. Lance Corporal Coltman immediately removed the bombs and Very-lights;

'7 June 1917. The Company HQ was set on fire by a trench mortar bomb causing several casualties. Lance Corporal Coltman tended the wounded and amongst others bound up one with both legs broken;

'14 June 1917. A tunnel through an embankment was blown in and 12 men buried. He immediately organised a party to dig out the buried men and supervised the removal of the wounded and was undoubtedly responsible for saving the lives of several men.'

Nine days later the *London Gazette* of 25 August 1917 announced the award of the Distinguished Conduct Medal 'For most conspicuous gallantry and devotion to duty during operations south-west of Lens between 28 June and 2 July 1917. Lance Corporal Coltman's conduct was magnificent.'

On 6 January 1919, the *Gazette* announced the award of the Victoria Cross 'For most conspicuous bravery, initiative and devotion to duty. During the operations at Mannequin Hill, NE of Sequehart, on 3 and 4 October 1918, Lance Corporal Coltman, a stretcher-bearer, hearing that wounded had been left behind during a retirement, on his own initiative went forward alone in the face of fierce enfilade fire, found the wounded, dressed them, and on three successive occasions carried comrades on his back to safety, thus saving their lives.

'This very gallant NCO tended the wounded unceasingly for 48 hours. He assisted in evacuating several badly wounded men from the front line and working untiringly until every wounded man had been taken out;

undoubtedly saving the lives of several of these men, as otherwise they would have had to lie up in the front line without proper attention [...] Lance Corporal Coltman's absolute indifference to danger and his gallant conduct had an inspiring effect on the rest of the men and was a splendid example to all. I cannot speak too highly of this NCO's gallantry on this and many previous occasions.'

When Coltman was invested with his Victoria Cross by King George V at Buckingham Palace on 22 May 1919, the King told him, 'Yours is one of the very few, if not the only case in the whole British Army, where a man has gained so many distinctions. I heartily congratulate you.' After the investiture, Coltman was granted leave but left the train before its arrival in his home town of Burton because he wanted to avoid the back-slapping planned by some civic dignitaries. He had, he said later, already had all the recognition due to him.

Yet even this was not his last trip to the Palace. That December, the *Gazette* announced a bar to his Distinguished Conduct Medal. 'On 28 September 1918 near Bellinglise,' it reported, 'this Lance Corporal dressed and carried many wounded men under heavy artillery fire. The following day, during our advance, he remained at his work without rest or sleep, attending the wounded, heedless of shell and machine-gun fire and never resting till he was positive that our sector was clear of wounded. In addition he was a most valuable means of communication, bringing back with his wounded accurate information of the advance. In spite of very thick smoke and fog he always found his way and so far as his work allowed, served as a guide. He set the very highest example of fearlessness and devotion to duty.'

Shortly before his death at the age of 83, Coltman said, 'I sincerely hope that future generations will know nothing of war – only what they read in books – and never again will there come a time when a Victoria Cross can be won.' It remained his greatest pride that the most heroic soldier of the World War I was one who never fired a shot.

It is a curious fact that the most dangerous task is that given to those whose focus is not to kill but to save. When enemy fire is pouring down, the infantryman can go to ground behind cover and stay down. No medic can ever ignore the cries of the wounded. They have a different job to do. The army decrees that women cannot serve as infantry soldiers. They can, though, serve in the front line as medics. On 11 June 2006, C Company of 1st Battalion, Princess of Wales's Royal Regiment from The Queen's Royal Hussars Battle Group were deployed in support of the Iraqi Security Forces on a search operation in Al Amarah, southern Iraq. Aboard one of the Warrior armoured personnel carriers was 19-year-old Private Michelle Norris of the Royal Army Medical Corps. When she had arrived in April, the 5-foot tall medic had instantly been nicknamed 'Chuck' after the action movie star and by June had become part of the team, although the worst thing she had treated thus far had been an infected mosquito bite.

A year after joining up, she was cramped in the stifling heat of the Warrior as it paused to help recover a vehicle that had become stuck in a ditch. As she sat waiting for the patrol to move off, she heard a noise. Then another. 'When I heard "dings" off the Warrior, I thought it was stones,' she recalls. It wasn't unusual for children to hurl stones as the armoured vehicles passed but it quickly became obvious that this was something else. In fact, insurgents had opened fire on them from five separate positions. It would become what the Ministry of Defence would later describe as a 'heavy, accurate and sustained attack from a well-organised enemy force of over 200' and the largest and most intense battle in Iraq since 2004.

Above her, the vehicle commander, Colour Sergeant Ian Page, stood in the turret of the vehicle in an attempt to locate the enemy positions until a round smacked through his rifle and into his face. In the vehicle's interior below him, Norris could see nothing. 'All of a sudden, the driver shouted down to me that my commander had been hit. It was my first casualty since training, which was pretty scary [...] At the time I knew someone needed help so I went out there and did what I could. In training you always get told to assess the situation first and then, if it's safe to do so, to go forward. But that day I didn't think about my own safety. I just knew I had to get him. I suppose I knew there were bullets, but I didn't know how many and you don't think, "I need to be brave", you think, "I just need to get to him". I was more worried about whether I would remember all the training and do the right thing, but it did all come rushing back to me. I remember the gunner yelling at me to get down. I heard rounds come whizzing past my head and I thought, "Yes, I probably do need to get down now" [but] before I could move he grabbed me and dragged me down into the vehicle.'

As the official report explains, 'Private Norris realised the severity of the situation immediately and without thought or care for her own personal safety, she dismounted and climbed onto the top of the Warrior to administer life-saving first aid to the casualty. On seeing her on the top of the Warrior the sniper opened fire again, firing a further three rounds at her, one hitting the radio mounted on the side of the turret inches from her leg.' Once the crew had managed to pull the casualty back inside and she had stabilised the wounds, Norris needed to prevent him going into shock. Since she joined the battalion, Sergeant Page had 'been like a father' to her and 'I just talked to him, I just kept saying, "Dad, are you with me? Dad, stay with me" until we got him to the casualty helicopter.'

Circling nearby was a Lynx helicopter of 847 Naval Air Squadron flown by US Marine Corps Major William D. Chesarek Jr, flying for the British on an exchange programme. With him were his crewmen Lt David Williams of the Royal Navy and Royal Marine Lance Corporal Max Carter. The crew had been flying during the night to provide a radio link for the ground forces below. Hearing about Page's injuries over the radio, he decided to fly low over the area in an attempt to distract the gathering crowd and if possible, to engage the insurgent positions. Because the crowd was by now so close to the ground troops, he realised his door gunner could not open fire. Instead he began what was later officially described as a 'bold, harassing, very low level flight over the area in an attempt to disperse the crowd'. By doing so, he became the main target. Small arms fire was directed at the helicopter while ground troops watched as a rocket-propelled grenade passed just behind his aircraft.

'I had been in a couple of situations with troops in contact before,' Chesarek later said. 'I had a good idea of the kind of potential danger involved, but now I was listening to the individual commander on the ground. Someone was injured; what can we do?' As he circled, he called in air support and succeeded in driving the gunmen out of the area before making the decision as the only helicopter in the area to land and pick up the wounded man. 'My door gunner jumped out and picked up the injured soldier and put him in the helicopter,' Chesarek said. 'My other crew member had to stay, or we would have been overweight to fly.' Quickly, Norris and Page were flown to safety.

'It was only when I sat down later and thought about it,' Norris later admitted, 'that I realised how scary the whole thing had been.' Colour Sergeant Page recovered from his wounds. 'He's fine. He's got a bit of scarring on his face, but apart from that he's doing really well.' The two met later at a base in Germany as they handed in their body armour. 'He gave me a hug and a kiss and said thank you.'

On 21 March 2007 Michelle Norris became the first woman to win the Military Cross. 'I never thought I'd go down in history for something I did, I can't explain it, I really can't. It's well over my head. I'm really proud to be the first woman to get the MC.'

At Buckingham Palace alongside Norris that day, Major Chesarek became the first American since World War II to be awarded the Distinguished Flying Cross. 'I am greatly honoured,' he told reporters, 'and would like to accept this prestigious award for 847 NAS in memory of Lieutenant Commander Darren Chapman of the Royal Navy, Captain David Dobson of the Army Air Corps, and Marine Paul Collins, who were killed in action over Basra in May 2006. The awarded actions were only possible due to the combined effort of my combat crew. My greatest sense of achievement that day is in knowing the ground troops all made it home.'

Completing the mission and making it home is what it is all about. When Walter Tull, a former professional footballer and the British army's first black officer to command white troops, was killed in action during the 1918 Spring Offensive, his men made repeated efforts to recover his body until they had to be ordered to abandon the futile attempts. They knew he was dead, but they couldn't bear the thought of leaving him out there alone. Ninety years later, the thought of leaving a comrade to fall into Taliban hands was so appalling that it led to one of the most dramatic missions of the war so far.

'The pilots both slipped open their canopies. One of them was leaning out and he gave me the thumbs-up, as if to say, "Shall we go?" I thought, "Is he mad?" Did he expect me to swing my leg over the rocket pod and off we'd go, do the job and come back and it's as simple as that? As it turned out, he did.' For Captain Dave Rigg of the Royal Engineers, Warrant Officer Class 1 Colin Hearn, Marine Gary Robinson and Marine Chris Fraser-Perry, it was the start of a rescue attempt that would make news around the world.

In January 2007, Royal Marines in Afghanistan had taken part in Operation Clay, a four-day sweep launched on New Year's Day to enable repairs to be carried out on a hydroelectric dam in the north of Helmand. The Taliban had been disrupting repairs to turbines at the dam on the Helmand River which supplied power to nearly two million people and water to a number of irrigation projects. Over 100 marines of 42 Commando's M Company had attacked the Taliban in a training camp and other locations, including a cave complex. Keen to capitalise on the resulting disorganization of the enemy, the plan now was to attack the Taliban-held Jugroom Fort near Garmsir – their equivalent of the British army's Camp Bastion – with the intention, as Lieutenant Colonel Rory Bruce, spokesman for the Marines, explained to reporters, 'to show the insurgents that they are not safe anywhere, that we are able to reach out to them and attack whenever and wherever we choose, even where they think they are at their safest'.

It began at dawn on 15 January 2007, with marines from Z Company,

45 Commando mounted in lightly armoured Viking vehicles and supported by tanks from C Squadron of the Light Dragoons crossing the Helmand River to the south-west of the enemy position. Earlier, the Brigade Reconnaissance Force had secured the crossing point and once the marines were across, they dismounted from the Vikings to assault the Taliban position. The attack was supported by fire from 105mm howitzers, Apache gunship helicopters and strike aircraft. Earlier, I Company – a unit composed of marines from 3 Commando Brigade Royal Marines' Command Support Group – had, alongside the Afghan National Police, conducted an attack north of the fort.

Despite the positive spin in press briefings, the operation was in difficulty from the start. A board of inquiry report later released by the Ministry of Defence exposed a series of errors, showing how a request for more troops by the commander of 3 Commando Brigade was turned down and how communications became confused as troops struggled to cope with unfamiliar equipment. The brigade commander had, it was revealed, identified 'shortfalls in combat power' that would prevent the British forces from succeeding in their goal to 'take and subsequently hold' ground. Pre-deployment training was geared too much towards old-fashioned peacekeeping operations and the marines were 'forced to adapt to a fast-moving operational environment quite different to that for which they had trained [...] Lessons were learned the hard way.'

As the marines charged towards the fort, they came under heavy fire. The briefing for the Viking crews had been rushed. A machine gunner on one of the vehicles opened fire. 'Thinking he had seen a muzzle flash,' the report explained, '[he] swung his weapon round almost 180 degrees and opened fire in the direction of the flash. Almost immediately the troops [...] began shouting at him to stop firing towards the wall, as did his driver.' In the chaos, 30-year-old Lance Corporal Mathew Ford was hit. 'In hindsight, it is highly likely that L/Cpl Ford had already – instantaneously – died from his wounds,' the report concludes. Both of his wounds, it adds, 'were very probably caused by NATO rounds'.

As the marines regrouped and a casevac Chinook helicopter was called in to pick up the wounded, they realised Ford was missing. An unmanned aerial probe was diverted to Jugroom and its operators noticed a figure lying just outside the fort's imposing walls. It was Ford.

Captain Charlotte Madison, the first woman to qualify as an Apache gunship pilot, was one of those scrambled to escort the Chinook. As the flight headed for Jugroom, the news reached them that the marines had a man missing. It was a scenario everyone dreaded. Not only would a captured British soldier be a propaganda coup, but it was more than likely that he would not survive the experience.

As the flight arrived, a plan was hastily devised using an as yet untried emergency rescue drill to allow downed Apache crews to be picked up by their wingman. The two-seater aircraft had no room inside, but it was just possible for two people to cling to the fuselage long enough to clear the immediate area of threat. If it could be used to extract people, it could also be used to insert them.

The plan was put to the marine's commander. Dave Rigg recalled: 'The Apache pilots recommended going in a pair, with two blokes hanging on to the sides of the helicopters. They would fly into position, the four blokes would jump off, grab Ford and then everyone would fly off again. It seemed an extraordinary, almost unbelievable plan. For one thing, I had no idea you could put passengers on an Apache. Where were they going to be? Hanging underneath it? Sitting on the side of it? But the pilots seemed confident.' Without explaining the plan, four volunteers were requested from men not immediately needed to man the Command Post. 'Without really thinking about it, a handful of people, including myself, volunteered. It was pretty instinctive really.'

Marine Gary Robertson had just entered the Command Post and immediately volunteered. A friend of Ford's, he 'just wanted to get him back'. Sergeant Major Colin Hearn said later, 'He's a Royal Marine the same as me – there was no way we were ever going to leave him, or anyone else, on that battlefield.'

The fourth man was Marine Chris Fraser-Perry, who had just woken up and was making himself some tea. He was asked if he would go and agreed without a second thought – although he didn't know what he had volunteered to do. 'I felt it had to be done. I would expect the same done for me.'

'I looked at the three men in front of me. Despite being a bit bewildered, they were all raring to go', Rigg explained. 'Everyone wanted to help, but it was the four of us who had been selected to do the job. We didn't want to let anyone down. I said, "Okay, do you know what we're going to do?" "No sir," came the reply from all three men.'

A quick briefing followed before the men ran to the waiting Apaches and tied themselves to the handholds above the helicopters' rocket pods. Trying to hold on as the helicopters took off in a swirl of dust, the four men were extremely vulnerable to small arms fire as they crossed the lines and headed for the fort's walls where Ford lay. In the choking dust, one helicopter overshot the outer wall so that when the marines jumped off, they headed towards what was actually the inner wall.

Above them, two more Apaches gave covering fire. In her book on her experiences in Afghanistan, *Dressed to Kill*, Charlotte Madison wrote:

Our Apache is to provide covering fire. But as we go in suddenly Face [one of the pilots on the ground] is really shouting. He must be in a bad way. 'I'm a sitting duck, I'm a sitting duck.' Face's voice penetrates my skull.

'I fire two missiles at point-blank range into the room at the fort where muzzle flashes are spitting. They stop and we reset just as Face says: 'They're firing again. I can't get them with my gun.' One enemy Rocket Propelled Grenade. That's all it would take.

'I struggle to get the missiles off at such close quarters. 'Get some f*cking fire down!' my colleague, Darwin, is shouting from the back seat. I'm wildly squeezing the trigger.

'After sending another missile through the roof of the building, our final one slams into a window and the firing stops. We fly underneath the blanket of smog – the scene looks like a macabre cartoon of a war zone: rubble, smoke, tracer, tiny bodies and plumes of angry fire.

'What a mess. Only our rockets left now. We set up for a run just to the east of where the two rescue Apaches are still sitting on the ground. I long to look but can't spare the concentration. We fire half our rockets, then repeat the manoeuvre to the north. They come out shooting in pairs, with their arses on fire. Suddenly an enemy RPG shoots past my window. 'What the f*ck? F*ck, help, f*ck!'

In the confusion on the ground, one of the Apache crew realised what had happened and jumped out to bring back the two marines as all three were is serious danger of being overrun by the Taliban. 'Face' sat helpless. As his colleague got out of the aircraft, he had locked the controls. If he didn't get back, the aircraft would stand no chance against a ground attack.

The second Apache team had landed about 70m from Ford but in the soft sand and heavy fire carrying the large marine, laden with his equipment, progress was slow. 'We thought we could land our two aircraft with four marines strapped on the side, grab Mathew and get back in two-and-a-half minutes,' explained Ed Macy, one of the Apache crewmen. 'But the dust from landing was horrendous, like a foot of talcum powder, and the second aircraft had to land in the next field. When the dust settled, I saw two Marines stuck in a ditch with Mathew, who was a man mountain. I jumped out and we heaved him up, but our feet just sank in the field. I was pinned down by Mathew and could see muzzle flashes. The other pilot and his marines ran to help and the ground in front of them was erupting. I have no fear of dying, but I didn't want to die there. With another 5 metres to go, Carl, my pilot, powered up the aircraft and the dust provided cover, so we clipped Mathew on the footstep and got out.' Above them, Madison was firing directly into a treeline just 200 metres away.

Madison again:

My head spins and I realise we are barely higher than the trees. I can look through the windows of the nearby buildings. I send the final flechette rockets into the distance. Face's flight lifts off in a huge cloud of dust and grit. As soon as they're away, Darwin pulls max power and climbs away to 2,000ft.

'We're Winchester, I tell him, with a huge exhalation of pent-up breath. It means we're out of ammo. [The saying is from World War I when biplane pilots had nothing left to fire and reached for their Winchester repeater rifles.] No one had yet gone Winchester in an Apache.

'Hello Five Two, this is Five Three pulling up, Winchester,' I tell my flight commander, Nick. 'Blimey. Not bad for a six-minute sortie,' he replies.

[As the helicopters returned, it was clear to the watching marines that Ford was already dead. His body was flown back to Camp Bastion by the waiting Chinook.]

Back on the ground, we find out Mathew Ford didn't make it. The knowledge sits heavily with me. It just seems so unfair.

A week later I walk into the squadron rest tent and the TV is on. A few people are crowded around watching. It is a documentary about the lives of some of the Marines out here. It takes me a while to realise that the lively, funny, healthy-looking man on the screen is the one who died in an instant, before my eyes, behind a dusty outhouse. It is like a punch in the stomach. I long to reach into the TV screen and pull out his smiling, brave, handsome face.

'Nausea rushes through me and I want to scratch at my skin. I feel horribly unsteady on my feet. I have to get fresh air. Resting my head in my hands, I tell myself to hold it together.

The following day, the marines held a service in memory of Ford. 'By now I had taken in the enormity of what we had done,' wrote Rigg. 'Some people might wonder why we went to such lengths to recover the body even when I suspected he was dead. But once we had set out on our mission, we never once considered pulling out. Leaving our own in enemy hands was inconceivable; we were utterly determined to bring him back [...] It would have sent a very bad message to our soldiers had we left one of our own behind to the mercy of the Taliban.'

During the rescue, Rigg's weapon had repeatedly struck Ford's head so he unstrapped the weapon and put it to one side, but in the confusion left it behind. He took a lot of stick for that and 'I even had to complete a police report: the Royal Military Police wanted to know why I hadn't recovered it. In response I asked them why they hadn't visited the scene of the "crime".'

'While the death of Lance Corporal Ford was a tragic incident, the courage and professionalism of those men who recovered his body was exemplary and in the best traditions of the UK's armed forces,' said Bob Ainsworth, the armed forces minister.

The pilots found themselves initially facing disciplinary action for endangering their aircraft, but instead the two pilots received the Distinguished Flying Cross, their co-pilots and Dave Rigg all won the Military Cross. The three marines received no recognition. The decision sparked a fierce internet debate on ex-service forums where some suggested such heroism was nothing out of the ordinary for the marines. One former sailor calling himself 'Ancient Mariner' wrote: 'I believe it's covered in week seven of the [Royal Marines'] course at Lympstone, just after the "leaping over tall buildings in a single bound" module and before they learn to make bullets bounce off their chest.' One former marine, though, said that at the end of the day the medals were unimportant. 'What is worth more, to become a corps legend and go down in history as "one of those nutters on the Apaches", or a medal?'

However they are remembered, the message went out to everyone in the military: whatever happens, we will come for you.

CHAPTER EIGHT
THE BATTLE OF GARMSIR
7–8 SEPTEMBER 2007

Military historians make a distinction when discussing the various types of action a soldier might find himself in. A 'battle' is usually regarded as a planned affair, both sides manoeuvring their forces to gain the advantage. Far more common, though, is the 'skirmish', a small-scale encounter that will rarely be remembered by anyone who wasn't part of it. The following account is taken largely from the report by *Guardian* Special Correspondent Audrey Gillan published in January 2008. It describes just one of the hundreds of firefights British soldiers have found themselves involved in during the war in Afghanistan:

Their six-month tour was almost over. This was their final mission. But over the course of one night, A (Grenadier) Company would undergo one of the most intense firefights of the war in Afghanistan. They had bartered with the local Afghans, swapping pens for cooking oil, potatoes and cans of Coca-Cola. This was the last supper, they joked, and the chips, fried in large ammunition tins set over flammable blocks, were, they said, 'the sweetest you could ever taste'. That night's operation – to push the Taliban farther south towards the Pakistani border – would be their very last of the tour, before the next day's handover to the Grenadier Guards. It would end up being one of the most intense single firefights undergone by any British army unit serving in Afghanistan in the past six years, leaving two soldiers dead and seven injured, three very seriously.

The next day A (Grenadier) Company, the 2nd Battalion, the Mercian Regiment (Worcesters and Foresters), was due to leave the perilous Garmsir area in southern Helmand province and fly up to the relative comfort and safety of the British army base at Camp Bastion. From there they would fly home, bringing to an end their six-month tour. A Company was close-knit, but the lads of 1 Platoon felt they had such a special bond they nicknamed themselves the Spartans, 'because we really are warriors'. Some had gone as far as burning an S into their calves, their branding tool improvised with scavenged wire heated over a naked flame, videoing the ceremony for posterity.

Most of the soldiers had just come into Forward Operating Base Delhi after weeks in outlying positions where they were being shot at and rocketed around 10 to 15 times a day. Out there they slept in their body armour, so the chance to pull on flip-flops and shorts and take a breather in the 50C heat was a relief. Some helped with peeling the potatoes, others sat around listening to iPods, fiddling with night vision equipment or just taking some quiet time out. But the atmosphere was a little edgy: a soldier becomes more superstitious during the final days. 'It's like going to a casino; every time you roll the dice, you're raising the probability of getting hit. Towards the end of a tour, you get probability compression,' says Major Simon Boyle, the company's current commander. 'You don't want to be the last bloke to die.'

After eating, it was time to get ready for battle. They got kitted up and camouflaged their faces with green, brown and black paint. As they waited, Private Matthew Carlin tried to boost morale [...] 'We all formed a circle, about 40 of us, and everyone who wanted to make a tit of themselves got in the circle and started break-dancing and stuff in the sand, and everyone was there whistling with their head torches flashing on and off, creating a sort of disco. I would stand in the middle and shout it out, and the whole company would repeat it back, with clapping effects as well.'

The officers and NCOs stood on the sidelines, smiling at the soldiers, many of them just 18 years old, as they took turns to rap and break-dance to the crowd. 'I was the party pooper who had to tell them to get their kit sorted and do a last-minute check on them,' says Lockett, 27. 'I checked the numbers. Suddenly the mood was very quiet and battle discipline was at a maximum. As we left camp, I shouted, "You all right, lads, everything all right? Happy days."'

It was last light on Saturday 7 September 2007 when A Company marched out of the gates of their base with three platoons of between 22 and 25 soldiers each. Their mission, Operation Pechtaw, was part of a bigger push on the Taliban, which would take the British army farther south than it had ever been – with 1 Platoon at the head. The Garmsir area is close to the border with Pakistan, and the Taliban is said to use this frontier as a blooding ground for new fighters before they are moved north to the Upper Sangin Valley.

'Down there, it's a lot like World War I, with our forward lines, the enemy forward lines and no man's land. The enemy would come into no man's land to attack us,' says 1 Platoon commander, Lieutenant Simon Cupples, aged 25 and also known as Boss. 'We would go to the edge of no man's land to the enemy's forward line, clear it and destroy it. The aim was to push back the Taliban and make it safer for the British taking over from us in Garmsir.'

They had to go less than 1km from base, but it was pitch black and there were massive irrigation ditches to negotiate. Fanning out, the platoons began clearing deserted farms and old agricultural compounds, moving west to east from locations they dubbed Stripped Wood and Three Walls towards Snowdon, a large hill from where the Taliban had launched numerous attacks over the past six months and where they were believed to keep weapons and ammunition. On the southernmost flank was 1 Platoon. It was nearly midnight. Having reached no man's land, they had just gone firm, positioning themselves flat on the ground, when machine guns opened up on them from 30 metres away. Four men in the seven-man section, including the section commander, Corporal Lee Weston, were directly hit. Others were temporarily blinded by phosphorus and disoriented. It was nearing midnight.

'The weight of fire was just horrendous,' said Jonathon McEwan, 'you were very lucky if you didn't get hit. I remember crawling back with the bullets literally just inches from your head.'

Not only were they being attacked by bullets and rocket-propelled grenades, but the Taliban were hitting the platoon with 'some kind of Chinese firecracker, like a catherine wheel'. The air filled with smoke and sand billowed up. The soldiers could see nothing – when Cupples put down his rifle for a second, he had to grope to find it again. Then, just when he didn't want to be seen, the Taliban would fire over a mini-flare to illuminate their targets. Cupples laughs now at the memory: 'I had to stamp them out with my boot, and I was thinking, "This is crazy, I'm fighting for my life and I'm trying to put out a fire."'

Lockett recalls: 'There were people going everywhere. You don't know if they are falling over or getting down, you don't know what's going on. There were five or 10 seconds of massive confusion. The next thing I know, I'm being picked up off the ground – I had been knocked unconscious. The rounds were literally going past my face. I remember getting back up and not being able to see anything and then my vision slowly coming round.'

Carlin was next to him and when he saw Lockett going down he thought he had been hit. 'The only way I can describe it is like being in a car crash, but the feeling lasted for hours and you can't get rid of it. I really thought I was going to die. The enemy fire was unbelievable. Everyone thinks the Taliban are just some bums with AK47s, but they are really good soldiers.'

The ferocity of the Taliban's attack had taken them all aback. Cupples went straight on to his radio, desperately telling his commanding officer back at base what was happening, trying to work out which of his men were down and where. 'Suddenly we were in the enemy's killing area. The bullets were winging everywhere.'

'I knew immediately we had soldiers hit,' Cupples later recalled. 'You could tell from the screaming and shouting. I knew how close the enemy were because you could hear the weapons going off and you could see the flashes of the muzzle as they were fired. To my right I could hear screaming, to my left mumbling. My Corporal had had his helmet blown off his head by an RPG.

Everyone was shouting and screaming to get back. Private Johan Botha, a South African who had joined the British army four years earlier, could not be located. Nor could his fellow soldiers, privates Sam Cooper and Luke Cole.

Over the screaming chaos, soldiers remember Botha's distinctive Afrikaans accent on their personal role radios [PRR], shouting, 'Boss, please don't leave me.' Lieutenant Rupert Bowers, a 20-year-old second lieutenant who had finished training just before arriving in Afghanistan the week before the attack, and who had joined the platoon three days earlier, was shadowing Cupples. He heard the call. 'That was quite a distressing thing. One of the first things I did was close my eyes for two seconds and said, "Please God, let me live."'

Cole, who had been shot in the leg, could also be heard shrieking 'They're coming to get him.' Cole – a Territorial Army soldier who was a forklift truck engineer back home – later described how he could see shadows moving and, convinced the Taliban were trying to pull Botha away to their trench, he kept shooting. 'I saw the muzzle flash from a single-shot weapon,' Bowers says. 'I got down on to my knee, the Taliban illuminated himself with his own muzzle. I fired two shots. I heard screaming, then he stopped.'

Beside him, Corporal Ben Umney was reeling after a bullet pierced his helmet and, somehow, stopped short of his skull. Bowers gave him his weapon and set about throwing water into the eyes of privates Kyle Drury and Ben Johnston to get rid of the phosphorus, before dragging them into a ditch.

In that ditch lay Lockett, massively disoriented. 'Everything was just crazy,' he says. 'I spent a good 10–15 minutes accounting for people. I was literally on my back at this time. I just kept talking to my blokes, saying, "We're all right, keep your f*cking heads down, lads, and wait out for my QBOs [quick battle orders]." I told all of them to check fire – I must have shouted it about 30 times – because we didn't know where any of our lads were and we didn't want a blue-on-blue [friendly-fire incident]. I knew I had casualties and I had to sort out the casevac party. I went down the line shouting for volunteers, but I didn't want to take too many men out and lose men to retrieve men.'

While Lockett tried to account for casualties in the ditch, Cupples was still out in no man's land, looking for Cooper, Cole and Botha. Being a commander, it was imperative he moved away from the front of the front line.

'I saw Mr Cupples on my left side and he started to say, "crawl towards me, crawl towards me,"' said Cole. At that moment the private was shot again, in the stomach, leaving his bowels protruding. 'I shouted to him, "Sir, I've had enough now. I'm not doing any more."'

'He was crawling slowly away from the enemy,' Cupples says. 'He was saying, "Look, I can't do it." I was encouraging him to talk, but he's now shouting and drawing fire, and I had to tell him to shut the f*ck up.'

Lockett roared at Cupples through the PRR that he had to come back to the ditch and reassess from there. 'But I didn't want to leave three blokes on the ground. I said to Cole, "Don't worry, I'm sorting it out for you, we have got other sections that are coming to help us." I had to tell him I was going. For someone injured, to see the platoon commander get up and run off, that would distress him a lot. I said, "Don't worry, I'm coming back for you, keep your rifle with you, I won't be gone long." It's quite a hard thing to do. You're then leaving him to fend for himself, and he is very close to the enemy [...] For him to see his platoon commander get up and run away from him. It must have been an awful thing to see.'

'I just wanted to get out of there,' said Cole. 'So, when he says "I'll be back for you, don't you worry, I'll be back for you," I thought, "Oh, all right then." It felt like a lifetime. It was horrible. I was on my own.'

When Cupples got back to the ditch, Lockett had the rescue party sorted out. Lockett and Bowers were to go together and Cupples would take Lance Corporals Jonathan McEwan and David Chandler. 'It's your mates out there,' said Corporal McEwan. 'All you wanted to do was get your mates out. Because if you'd seen them, well if Private Botha had got dragged in by the Taliban, I couldn't have lived with that.' They all moved forward in a 'run, crawl, walk'. Lockett describes it: 'We would run and draw fire. It was inevitable they were going to see us coming. We needed to cover as much ground as fast as we could. So it was literally a mad dash for it, then get down and start crawling.'

'I could see everything that was going on,' Cole remembers. He was using his radio to describe the movements of the enemy just metres away. 'I could see the Taliban. You could hear them laughing and passing on commands all around. I could see them trying to grab my mate and I thought "That can't be" so I carried on firing. You knew for a fact they were trying their hardest to get to you but they couldn't get to you.'

Lockett and Bowers spotted Cooper and Cole 30 to 40 metres away. Zigzagging to avoid gunfire, they ran towards them. Lockett says, 'I was shouting to Cole, "Get the f*ck over here, you need to get the f*ck over here." I was absolutely f*cking gobbing at him, egging him on. He was making his way towards me with a morphine autojet, shouting, "Put this in me," but he wasn't a massive casualty at this point and I was saying, "No, I haven't got f*cking time, I've got fire coming in and I've got to get Cooper. As soon as we get 10m away, I will smash you with that morphine." If we moved, we were going to get hit. I had a lifespan of about two seconds there.'

Cooper, the youngest soldier in the regiment having only just turned 18, looked dead. Bowers had him by the hand, which was stone-cold, and he could smell blood. 'We were shaking him and there was a bit of gurgling and he didn't look f*cking good,' Lockett says. He got his Leatherman knife out of his pocket and began cutting off Cooper's kit. Then Bowers, a tall, thin man, got ready to take the private's limp body on his shoulders. 'I thought "I'm going to have to sacrifice security and safety for efficiency" and I just got up and ran for it. I knew when I stood up I was going to start making myself a target but it was something I thought was necessary. There's a man who's still alive and he wasn't going to be for much longer if I didn't get help [...] Just as I got up to run, a bullet came really close. I did a weird sort of crawling motion, then stood up again and ran with him on my back. Another bullet came dangerously close and I went face first. I got him to the ditch. Me and Corporal Umney then tried to get a response out of Cooper. I said, "Cooper, have you got a girlfriend?" Someone said, "Has she got big tits?" And he lashed out and punched Umney – that was the only response he gave that night.'

Behind him, Corporal McEwan was still with Cole. He and Chandler were dragging him by straps on his equipment. 'Up for a few seconds then hit the deck again. Then go through the whole process again. Constantly having to talk to Cole because he was in and out of consciousness all the time. I thought he was dead but he kept coming back.' After what seemed hours, they reached the ditch where Cole was given morphine. The company medic, Private Lee Stacey, looked at Cooper's head and saw the extent of his injuries. Some of his brain seemed to be protruding from his skull. Having pushed it back in, Stacey wound the bandage round and then Bowers dragged him back the short distance to Three Walls.

Three Walls was comprised of three low mud walls, the remnants of a compound that provided a little shelter behind their forward lines. At one point about 50 men were using it to take cover. [...]

Sergeant Major Peter Lewis and the company doctor arrived at the scene in Viking armoured personnel carriers. Lewis had brought more ammunition as it was running short on the field. They began extracting casualties, triaging them from T1 (life-threatening injuries), to T3 (walking casualties). So far there were no T4s: dead.

Back at the ditch, Cupples was calling in fire support and mortars, with the intention of clearing the Taliban trench. But, landing only 20 metres away, the rounds were heart-stoppingly close. 'At this point, the enemy was starting to regroup. I knew they were hurting quite a lot now, but they had got the upper hand initially. We had superior firepower support, too. We could hear them screaming [...] At this point the firing slowed down. You could hear a lot of movement in their trenches, you could hear them coming round to the left, that's when they were trying to outflank us. Now that they were trying to regroup, the risk became too great – we didn't have enough firepower to cover us.'

Back at base Major Jamie Nowell, commander of A Company, asked 3 Platoon to provide covering fire and to extract Botha from the killing zone, dead or alive. 'At that time we classed him missing in action,' Cupples says. 'We just didn't know.'

Craig Brelsford was 3 Platoon's sergeant – Lockett's opposite number and a friend. 'I said to him, "Brelsy, mate, Botha is up there, can you bring the big man back for me?" He's like, "Don't worry, we'll get him." I promised at the beginning of that tour that I would bring everyone back. [...] I wanted them to think, "If anything happens, I'll be all right, Locky will be here in seconds,"' Lockett says.

Three or four minutes later the shout went out, 'Man down, man down', over the radio. Brelsford had been shot [fatally] in the neck. Meanwhile, air support had been called in to drop 500lb bombs on the Taliban positions, and A Company had 10–15 seconds to get under cover. 'We were sat against the wall, with our heads between our knees and they gave us a quick countdown,' Lockett says. 'All you can hear are the massive screeches of the planes coming in. It's low and it's fast and you'll not see [them]; it's a blur. The second 500-pounder had knocked a bit of wall off and it landed on Stacey's neck. Next thing we heard "man down, man down". Stacey had been hit. He was walking and we got him on the Viking and out of harm's way.'

They were ordered to retreat to base. It was almost 6.30am and light was approaching. Even with the use of thermal sights, aircraft could see no sign of Botha's body. It was feared that the private was now in the Taliban trench or held captive.

Back at camp, the soldiers took off their body armour and helmets. 'I had 25 of my platoon walk out the gate that night and I had 16 walk back in – I had lost Botha and eight of my boys were injured,' Lockett says. 'The lads split up into their own little groups. I could see that everyone was massively upset. We didn't know where Botha was.'

Lockett gathered his soldiers around him. 'I said, "Right, boys, close in, I need eight volunteers to go out and bring the big man back. If you don't want to come out, I will fully understand, but bear in mind he went out there with you." Nearly everyone volunteered.'

Cupples commanded the first of three rescue Vikings. 'You had to be out of your mind to want to go back into that area to fight. It's a lot for the blokes to do. They only do it because it's one of their own men. They know there could be some kind of trap, that Botha could be booby-trapped or the enemy could be watching him and waiting for us to come back.'

At 7.30am they went back for Botha. Carlin was in the back of one Viking, part of the snatch team that would, should Botha be located, burst out of the back door and pull him inside. Lewis was expecting hell. 'I was almost certain we were going to get some of the same ferociousness when we opened the door.' But there was none. The bombs seemed to have done their job.

They found Botha's body about 20 metres from the Taliban trench. The ground was smoking. Botha was dead, still sitting in a firing position. 'We got him in the back of the Viking. The doctor just said, "Lads, he's T4. Sorry, lads, he's dead."'

Captain Henry Nwume, 30, the doctor, tried to resuscitate him, but Botha had no pulse and wasn't bleeding. 'He had dust on his cornea, which made me think he was dead because you would normally blink or you would tear it up. I told the sergeant major he was dead and one of the corporals started crying, then the other. It was a long journey back. Botha was lying at our feet. We started struggling around to get a poncho to put on him. It was 15 minutes of misery jammed in the back of the wagon with Botha's body. He had taken a round through the shoulder and through the arm [...] I remember the guys asking, "Do you think it was quick, Doc?" but I don't know.'

Sergeant Major Lewis thinks it was a job well done: 'It would have made a massive amount of difference if we had lost Botha's body. Getting him back was a massive, massive bonus. I would have been a lot more haunted than I am.'

After helping take Botha's body off the Viking, Carlin broke down for three hours. 'I just couldn't speak. Never felt anything like it. Every soldier wants a firefight in their corner, and that was mine, but I don't wish it on anyone for the feelings we went through that night.' Lewis and Lockett took the kit and weapons off Botha and Brelsford, before putting them in body bags and on to the helicopter to Camp Bastion. 'All the way through my army career I have been a stickler for kit and up until that op we had never lost any kit. That op, I think we lost two rifles and some night vision. I wasn't even worried about it. I just had two men dead, so the price of a rifle and some night vision was irrelevant to me,' Lewis says. The sergeant major is the last one who can break down in front of the men and it was difficult to keep it together. 'I found it hard not to release out there. I wanted to, but you've got to seem to be strong. I can only put it down to the same sort of feelings as when I lost my dad.' […] A Company were flown up to Camp Bastion the next day and arrived home in October.

When Gillan wrote the above account, 18-year-old Private Sam Cooper had suffered brain damage, was unable to speak and had limited movement down one side of his body. Private Luke Cole was alternately using a wheelchair and walking sticks, but he will never run again. Private Lee Stacey, who was attached to the platoon that night as both a gunner and a medic, had serious neck injuries which meant he would never serve again. The battlefield dead estimate for Taliban was put at nineteen.

'When he talks,' Gillan wrote, 'to stop himself crying again, Carlin plays with the rubber wristbands on his arm. One states: "Support Worcesters and Foresters in Afghanistan", the other, simply "Spartans". "At the start of the tour we were mates, but now we are like brothers," he says. "And in memory of my brothers, I will never take these off, unless someone has to take them off for me."'

Corporals Chandler and McEwan were both awarded Joint Commander's Commendations for their actions in rescuing Luke Cole. Second Lieutenant Rupert Bowers was Mentioned in Dispatches for his rescue of Sam Cooper. Private Luke Cole, 24, was awarded the Military Cross for his actions in covering his wounded comrades and reporting Taliban movements despite his own injuries. He was left permanently disabled by leg wounds and although he no longer uses a wheelchair, he is unable to return to his former job of fork-lift truck engineer. In 2009 he was undergoing retraining at a specialist college for the disabled.

Lieutenant Simon Cupples, 25, from Chesterfield, was awarded the Conspicuous Gallantry Cross, second only to the Victoria Cross. Now promoted to Captain, he is second in command of A (Grenadier) Company, 2 Mercians.

Of the rest of the platoon, Corporal Ben Umney left the army in 2009 after eleven years' service. He now runs his own plumbing business. Eighteen-year-old Private Sam Cooper suffered brain damage in the ambush, which affects his speech and one side of his body. Private Matthew Carlin has since left the army. Lance Corporal Lee Weston was shot and wounded in the shoulder during the night ambush. He has now left the army and is a qualified mechanic. Private Kyle Drury, 22, was temporarily blinded by phosphorus during the ambush and shot in the chest, but saved by his body armour as the bullets deflected off his radio. Since promoted to lance corporal, he is still in the army.

Private Ben Johnson, 23, was also temporarily blinded by phosphorus during the night ambush. He is still serving and has been on active service again in Helmand. Acting Sergeant Michael Lockett, then aged 27, was promoted to Sergeant. He received the Military Cross from the Queen at Buckingham Palace. He returned to Afghanistan in 2009 and was killed by an IED on the last day of his tour, only the second holder of the MC to be killed in action since World War II. He had volunteered to stay on at his patrol base to ensure that the incoming soldiers knew as much as they could about the local area. He left behind his three children from a former marriage, his own family and his girlfriend Belinda English, who, paying tribute to him later said simply: 'For Queen and Country.'

CHAPTER NINE

BEHIND THE LINES

The battlefield in the old days was a comparatively safe locality except at close quarters; but today death has a wider range and if the losses of a modern battle are relatively less, the strain on the nerves is more severe.

Colonel G.F.R. Henderson

One day in 1944, Bill Stafford received orders to move. 'When I got to Uxbridge I was escorted past dozens of Military Police drilling on the parade grounds to a second, much larger, camp at the rear. There were rather fewer personnel in evidence, but the place was crammed with every type motor vehicle that I had ever seen, and many that I had never seen before in my life. I was left in the [Station Warrant Officer's] office, where I was to learn that I was to join the 2nd Tactical Air Force advance party, which was gathering for the invasion of Europe. After intake procedures I was shown to a bed space in a Nissen hut and then taken to a room where I was to work for the remainder of my stay.'

After several false starts, Stafford found himself in 'one of the longest convoys the RAF had ever seen. I was travelling in a Water Bowser [with] just the driver and myself and we thought this was very comfortable, we were located in the middle of the convoy and the exhaust fumes were something else. Thank goodness we were not at the rear. We were going all day. Our destination turned out to be Gosport with its Mulberry Harbours.' They remained parked in a side street for several days until ordered to move on. 'We went like bats out of hell down to the nearby Mulberry docks where there were a large number of flat-bottomed Tank Landing craft awaiting us. We drove our wagons right on to the craft to the far end which was the stern. We then had to turn to and chain them down. Fumes, condensation, stench, perspiration, none of us escaped it. But this was nothing! The tanks followed us on, and we had to chain these down as well. The fumes and stench were multiplied tenfold and the condensation was dripping from the underside of the upper deck so much that it resembled being in a thunder storm. We were still completing these tasks when we set sail, and we did not see the leaving of our shores.'

'As we neared the Normandy coast we were ordered back on to our vehicles ready to disembark. A shudder went through the landing craft as we hit the beach, the ramps dropped down, the tanks thundered off and then it was our turn. Down the ramp and on to Juno beachhead.

'The first of our forces had landed about four or five days prior to us and the evidence of the hellish time that they had experienced was enough to make you sick. The beach was still littered with wrecked and abandoned tanks, trucks, jeeps, guns –even clothing and personal effects. Hundreds of army personnel were busy extricating gruesome remains out of some of the wreckage. Our sight of this was very brief: there was no stopping, across and up the beach into a very narrow country lane. Progress was rather slow, we had to be very cautious, our front line was still only about 6 or 7 miles ahead and we could hear the noise of gunfire up ahead. We had been going for no more than a mile or so when we were directed into a large field surrounded by trees. All the vehicles were driven under the trees for camouflage. Those with no tree used camouflage nets. We were warned to expect enemy aircraft raids at any time, especially at dusk and dawn and we were told to sleep under our vehicles to obtain what shelter we could. Because we had no time to dig in my driver and I thought, "Great, lucky us, riding on a water bowser: solid metal, safe as houses."

'Sure enough, just as dawn was breaking over comes Jerry and strafed us well and proper. There were no major casualties. Only two very soaking wet airmen. Jerry's bullets had pierced the bowser's walls and we got soaked. Laughing stocks the pair of us.

Later, as the battle progressed, the convoy set off on our new route. We then started to see at first hand the horror and destruction which the battles had left behind. Especially the towns of St-Lô and Vire. They had been completely flattened to the ground and were still smoking and burning in many places. Even so we still got the odd cheer from the very few people who were still to be seen rooting around in the rubble. I will never forget the smell of burning, and an indescribable stench of rotting flesh and other things.'

Stafford remained in the front lines until Christmas, when he became ill and was diagnosed with bronchial pneumonia. 'I did not respond to treatment [...] So it was decided to transfer me to a larger hospital outside of Brussels. On New Year's Day morning at about 8am I was on a stretcher being loaded into an ambulance when the sirens sounded and two Messerschmitt fighters came over and strafed us. Me and the stretcher were three parts of the way into the ambulance with bullets thudding into the ground all around us. The driver and his mate who were loading me dived under the ambulance, leaving me out to dry! I felt so rotten that, bullets or no bullets, I was not staying there. So I rolled off the stretcher, pulled it the rest of the way in and climbed back on. I was too sick and exhausted to give a damn.'

After his recovery, Stafford returned to his unit and stayed with them to the end of the war, eventually finding himself in 'a small but beautiful town which was in peace time a spa by the name of Bad Eilsen. We came to rest here, and here we stayed for the remainder of the war, ultimately becoming the British Air Forces of Occupation Operations (BAFO OPS). Running past the gable ends of the Furstenhoff Hotel [where HQ was based] was a road, with a wide grass bank sloping downwards, between it and the gable ends. Someone had found in this sloping bank a mass grave containing the bodies of eleven British servicemen. We had an officer in charge of intelligence who looked and acted as abrupt and domineering as any German officer that I have ever seen portrayed. He ordered every person in the town over ten years of age to be rounded up and herded to this mass grave. We in turn were made to line the road with fixed bayonets whilst these people, men women and children, were paraded past the open grave and were made to stop and view the mangled bodies [...] I felt sick, standing there with rifle and bayonet, because I knew that in many instances, force had to be used to induce some of them to come. It took a few days to clear up from this, the bodies were removed, the earth put back and re-grassed, until no signs remained.'

Landing on Juno Beach shortly after D-Day, advancing through the still smoking ruins of French towns, coming under air attack and finding a mass grave. A an adventurous war for a man whose job was solely to provide haircuts: Bill Stafford was an RAF barber.

Frontline soldiers like to complain about REMFs – the 'Rear Echelon Mother F*ckers' who sit in safety while they are under fire. In essence, it's a term that describes 'anyone further from the firing line than me'. But, as Colonel Henderson points out, the battlefields of today are no longer confined to a small space. Famously, sightseers picnicked on the hills around Napoleonic battles as men fought to the death. In those days, unlucky was the man hit by an enemy soldier's musket at 50 yards, and battle was at close quarters. Today, war spreads.

In September 1939, as Lord Gort and General Dill prepared to leave for France, the Chief of the Imperial General Staff, General Ironside, met with them. 'I told them of all my strategic ideas', Ironside said later, 'and I then made an appeal to them to see that their men and transport did not expose themselves to air attack. Anywhere behind the fighting line is the battle line. Nowhere is anybody safe. All must dig in and disperse themselves. This is particularly necessary amongst the Army Service Corps and the Army Ordnance Corps'. The advice was ignored. As a result, rear echelon troops took the heaviest casualties when the German breakthrough came. In 1982 the Scots Guards lost eight men in the battle for Mount Tumbledown on the Falklands, but the Task Force also lost eight Chinese civilian laundrymen recruited by the Royal Navy who were killed in attacks on their ships. Nowhere is ever truly safe.

Far behind the lines are another army. An army of parents, relatives and friends waiting for news. Ida Gregory, whose husband Albert had landed with the first wave of airborne troops at Pegasus Bridge on D-Day, later admitted, 'Being a wife of someone in the armed forces was a terrible ordeal, you did not know where they were, you did not know if they were safe, in fact you did not know if they were alive or dead.

'One of the worst things to happen during the war years was the arrival of a Post Office telegram boy on his red bicycle in the road or street, for then you knew someone who lived close to you was going to receive some bad news. I remember the day I heard the news about my husband, Albert. I saw the telegram boy turn into King Street, and everyone closed their doors and looked through their net curtains to see which house he would stop at. On this particular day, he knocked on my door. The telegram read that he had been wounded and was in a military hospital in Oxford; my heart was heavy, but at least he was alive.

'The local people gathered to help me and the next day I caught a train to Oxford in the search for my husband. After walking miles I approached the hospital I didn't want to go to – Head Injuries. I asked at the reception if they had a Lance Corporal Albert Gregory and to my dismay, they said they had. I approached the ward not knowing what to find, and was led to a bed surrounded by curtains. There he lay, his head shaved and with wires attached to a machine, his arms strapped to the side of the bed and a 6-inch safety pin from a kilt pushed through his tongue to stop him swallowing it. For several weeks he was in hospital, then he was transferred to a convalescent home, and at last he came home for a few weeks. When he joined the army, he was designated as A1, but now he was C3 and would not fight abroad again.'

For families at home, especially those in forces married quarters, the wait is agonising. Like Ida, they watch for the signs, breathing a sigh of guilty relief when it is their friends, not they, who will bear tonight's grief.

June and Brian Callus were living in Africa when the South Atlantic war began. Their youngest son, 24-year-old Paul was aboard HMS *Coventry*. Brian had retired from the Royal Navy in 1974 with the rank of Lieutenant Commander and was working as the electrical engineering manager of the Zambia Sugar Company at the time. 'We were listening to the BBC World Service and picked up the news that two destroyers had been hit. At that stage the names of the ships weren't released but we both had a terrible feeling. Then they disclosed that one of the ships was a sister ship of HMS *Sheffield*. Well, that narrowed it down to HMS *Coventry* or HMS *Glasgow*. Then on a much later bulletin they said it was *Coventry* and at that time we had absolutely no way of knowing whether Paul was a survivor or not.'

Their hopes were raised when a telex initially did not include their son on the list of casualties. 'I still had a pretty bad feeling about it,' Brian later admitted. 'The following morning when I went to work the general manager came into my office with a piece of paper and I could see from his face that it was bad news.' The casualty list had been revised and the last name on it was Paul's.

Brian drove back to his house to tell June. She only needed to take one look at her husband to know her worst fears had been confirmed. They immediately flew back to their home to comfort their two other sons, Stephen and Peter.

Brian returned to Zambia because he couldn't bear to watch the televised tumultuous homecoming welcome for the survivors. 'I would be looking at people celebrating their survival. I didn't begrudge them that

– but I didn't find it easy to cope with.' Even now, the couple are still tormented by feelings of guilt. 'Paul had spoken about leaving the navy and I wanted him to stay on longer to gain more experience,' Brian told *Portsmouth News* on the fifteenth anniversary of the war. 'When he was a young apprentice I remember him saying that he felt he was being well paid for what he was doing. And I remember telling him that one day he might well have to pay for it.' Today, a magnolia tree stands in the grounds of the local Roman Catholic church dedicated to the memory of a former altar boy who perished in the South Atlantic. It flowers in May, the anniversary of his death.

Watching and waiting is all the families can do. Roy McCallum, whose son Kelvin died aboard HMS *Glamorgan* during the Falklands conflict, has said, 'Anyone with a services background knows that if two padres come to your door it means there has been a death. If it's one, it means an injury. When I opened our door there were two on the step.

'It was his first ship,' Mr McCallum recalls. 'He need not have gone because his wife had not been too well during her pregnancy. But she was getting better. Kelvin only had about a month's remaining duty on *Glamorgan* and was only going to be away a couple of weeks. But the ship was sent from Gibraltar direct to the Falklands. We never saw our son again.' After an Exocet missile struck the ship just two days before the end of the war, he was among the 13 men killed. Kelvin was buried at sea.

Later, as Kelvin had wanted, his daughter – whose name he had chosen before sailing – was christened on board HMS *Glamorgan*. After the ceremony her grandfather went below to the hangar where his son had died. 'I let go. It was the first time I had cried and let it out. Kelvin was such a happy lad and so kind. Now his mother and me talk about him as if he is still with us. We say how much he would have liked a particular fashion or piece of music. And we only have to look at Gemma to see him.'

Since the first Zeppelin raids struck Britain in World War I, civilians have never again been safely removed from the battlefield. According to the

White House, between 1941 and 1945, the US Navy suffered a total of 36,950 battle deaths, the US Marine Corps some 19,733. By contrast, in the period 1939–45, British civilian casualties alone reached 67,073, over 60,000 by the time the first American troops entered Britain. In 1942, at Eisenhower's insistence, a guide was produced for American servicemen entering Britain. 'The British will welcome you as friends and Allies,' it told them. 'But remember that crossing the ocean doesn't automatically make you a hero. There are housewives in aprons and youngsters in knee pants in Britain who have lived through more high explosives in air raids than many soldiers saw in first class barrages in the last war.' Where possible, American bases ensured that on arrival men would be taken on a tour of bombsites to see what the locals had had to endure in the previous two years.

Aerial bombing took the war to civilians in their own homes and made the war personal for many at the front. Soldiers fought on the front lines only to hear that their families had died at home. War had moved from the isolated battlefield to a truly world-wide war. No longer could anyone truly consider themselves safe – not even the REMFs.

CHAPTER TEN
HACKING IT

Hack it: verb – To endure; to meet the challenge

The saying goes that war is 99 per cent boredom and 1 per cent terror. For the most part, it is a very personal battle to simply endure – to get through whatever is thrown at you and to go back home. It's often not the terror of battle men remember, but the small, day-to-day struggles.

In 1950, troops found themselves in conditions in Korea that would have been familiar to their fathers and grandfathers in World War I. 'I have two very vivid recollections', says veteran Peter Poole. 'Ask any veteran and they'll tell you – the cold! We were living in dugouts and tents, and it got down to minus 20, minus 30 – the winter in 1951 was particularly bad. But it was a dry cold. Crispy cold. Freezing cold! We relied very much on the Americans and Canadians, who provided us with extra food and clothing – they had much better equipment. The other thing you remember: the rats! With troops living in dugouts and trenches, and the way cans and foods were disposed of, it encouraged rats.'

For Major A.F. Campbell of the Suffolk Regiment, memories of Malaya are of 'arduous marching and back-breaking toil. Every day for two or three hours the rain beat down through the canopy of foliage 200 feet above our heads. It soaked through our clothes, through our skins, into the marrow of our bones. It turned the sand-soil floor of the jungle into a treacherous slippery quagmire. Our route lay across the grain of hilly country. We had to climb each ridge, dragging ourselves up the steep slopes, using hands, feet and knees and every muscle in our aching bodies to maintain balance and keep moving upwards. On reaching the top we would move along the ridge for a little way and then down the other side, slipping and sliding, clutching at every bush and sapling to prevent a headlong fall into the unseen raging torrent that crashed its way along the floor of the narrow valley below. On reaching the bottom, half-dead with fatigue, we must cross the stream, slowly feeling our way across the shifting boulders, hand-in-hand waist-deep in the madly rushing waters. And then, up again, over the next ridge. And at each step we had to fight the thick, clinging undergrowth, hacking a way through with machetes while thorns tore at us.'

In the breakout from San Carlos during the Falklands War, Jim Love and his unit were part of a 'snake' – a line of troops – as they climbed the line of the Sussex Mountains. 'It was a night move. For most of it a case of follow the leader. After the initial few hundred metres that got us off the reverse slope it was all down hill. That and on your arse. At first you tried to tab normally and follow the bloke in front. The standard battalion snake scenario. But it was not to be. The grass hummocks that went for miles due to the erosion of the soil and the eating habits of the islands' sheep caused maximum confusion. That, and lots of pain. You just couldn't get in a flow, that was the problem. Every couple of steps you tried a different method of coping with the terrain. We might have exercised on the sheep-filled hills of Wales, but apart from that there were f*ck-all similarities. The pace took its toll. We shuffled between the hummocks, but it tended to take you out of the snake and give the impression that you were walking further than necessary. You then tried to keep directly behind the guy in front. This caused you at times to jump from tussock to tussock, making the Bergen/radio on your back bounce up and down. Making you use more energy than necessary.

'We lost a few to ankle and foot- and leg-related injuries but the momentum carried on and now the war machine was at last moving up a gear. It was proving hard to keep up with the sense of urgency. Mind you, when we did manage to stop for a break, we tended to doze like all good soldiers do. The trouble was that when you woke up you couldn't quite remember where you were. I tended to think I was in the middle of Salisbury Plain on exercise.'

For some, it's the memory of long, agonising marches. For Ross Kemp, filming a documentary about British troops in Afghanistan, the simplest of daily routines became a test of endurance. 'Inside my chosen thunder box was a sheet of plywood with a seat and a metal drum underneath. The interior of the drum swarmed with flies, even at night. As I glanced into it with the light from my head torch, I saw what I can only describe as a mauve-brown porridge. The porridge was moving, thanks to the flies that had settled on it and were now feasting among the little white islands of toilet paper. [As I sat down] the flies swarmed up between my legs, one of them scoping out the moisture on the corner of my firmly closed mouth with the pinpoint accuracy of an F-16 Bomber. I knew perfectly well that the fly had just been dining on the porridge, so I flicked it away in a movement that must have made me look as if I was suffering some kind of muscular spasm.' That was at night. During the day, in 50-degree heat, the experience was far, far worse.

For the most part, war is neither exciting nor glamorous. The thunder boxes that greeted Ross Kemp have to be emptied daily and a soldier has to do it. Elsewhere, cooks prepare meals in kitchens where, with the heat outside already barely tolerable, the ovens create their own private hell. Surrounded by the enemy, the mundane daily routine continues, interrupted from time to time by IDF (indirect fire) of mortar and rockets fired indiscriminately into the camps.

Every camp needs supplies. Food, water, ammunition, mail from home. It all has to be carried to the front lines: 'Troops eat on the go, they pee on the go,' Captain Julie Booton told *Defence Magazine*. A reservist attached to 12 Logistic Support Regiment during its tour in Helmand, Captain Booton was responsible for monitoring the convoys and tracking their progress from Camp Bastion. Combat Logistic Patrols (CLPs), generally of 50 or more vehicles, leave the main British and US base at Camp Bastion every week or so and can be gone for a week at a time as they move from base to base. Major Joe Chestnutt, a regular convoy commander, explained: 'They can be very long trips – more than 40 hours [between camps]. We travel slowly because there are threats all along the routes. We carry out checks, which add time, as do any incidents along the way.' 'Even the girls are issued with bottles and "she-wees" [cardboard funnels],' said Captain Booton. 'Some of the female drivers were concerned at first, but we try to put them in cabs together. It's harsh but they get on with it and get used to it.'

The convoys set out under cover of darkness to try to minimise any immediate Taliban threat but travelling by night poses its own risk. It is much harder to spot any signs on the ground that might indicate the presence of an improvised explosive device. 'We can't just use the easiest routes, because that would make us an obvious target,' explained troop commander Lieutenant Dave Webster. Instead, the huge vehicles cross dried-up river beds and steep climbs over rough tracks. Dust and sand makes visibility poor and, Webster said, 'The soft desert sand makes manoeuvring very difficult. It makes it hard to see the vehicle in front, and also makes it hard to spot booby traps, even in daylight.' Accidents are frequent, as are attacks. Captain Guy Mason, responsible for planning CLPs, claims, 'It's not uncommon for a convoy to be hit by three or four IEDs during a patrol, and to come under small arms attack between 10 and 15 times. Generally, it is the vehicles that are damaged rather than the crews inside.'

War, wherever and whenever it is taking place, is not about battles, but about the long slog to victory. For the most part, soldiers don't care about medals and heroism, just in making it through another day. Cliff Billen was a 23-year-old Staff Sergeant and commander of a Sherman tank in the 11th Armoured Division during the Normandy campaign of 1944. He was involved in heavy fighting around the village of Tilly and here describes his experiences as his unit moved inland:

Leaving Tilly, and all the carnage behind us to other poor sods to sort out […] we moved on to the first major city of Caen, where the cream of Hitler's Panzer Divisions waited for us. As you will understand, it was our first real battle of any greatness. Finally we were able to enter Caen [less than 10 miles way] ten days later! Our battalion alone had lost 35 tanks out of 52.

It was there that I lost my first tank on the ninth day with the loss of my first driver – a lovely little lad from London. I wrote to his family – most of us carried letters in our pockets already addressed to home to be sent in the event of not making it – and in fact I did keep up a correspondence with them for a while after the war, but like all contacts, after a while it gets less and less and finally stops all together.

One evening when we had come back in for a rest [after] another lot had relieved us, I picked up a strange object in a trench that was shaped like a funnel. It had a double skin and three magnets on the base. We assumed that this was some sort of base for a radio mast and that the magnets would hold it in place. My driver asked me to take out the inner skin and then he could use it to refuel our tank a lot easier. This I did with a chisel and hammer [and] as I did so white powder came pouring out. I assumed it to be the insulation (bear in mind that I was sat by an open fire) that we had cooked on. The driver was more than pleased!

A few days later we were taken to see a selection of German mines so that we would know what to look for, and on the shelf – yes! there it was looking down at us!

'Oh Sergeant, that's not a mine on the top shelf, is it?'
'Oh yes my son, that is the latest anti-tank mine. They creep up and clamp them on the side with the magnets on the base.'

I went cold and looking at my driver, I thought that he was going to pass out! So I asked the Sergeant: 'What was the white stuff inside then?' and he replied, 'Oh that was the explosive. Hang on, how do you know there is white stuff inside?' So I told him what I had done. It was then his turn to go white! I always remember his words to me: 'You are telling me that you opened up an anti-tank mine with a hammer and chisel, tipped all the explosive out onto the ground alongside an open fire? My son, that is just not possible and live!' I am sure that he relates that story to this day – if he made it back.

As the Allies pushed inland, British armoured divisions swept through northern France and Belgium at a rate so fast that they were forced to plunder schoolrooms and local garages for maps to find out where they were. By early September, Cliff was on the Dutch border.

We had been travelling for about 30/40 miles this particular day, not meeting with much resistance at all, but we were praying that we would get orders to stop to rest up, feed etc. My new replacement driver was very good and a likeable lad from Scotland. The day before he had received a 'Dear John' letter from his wife [saying she had met someone else] of only one year. Quite a few were captivated by the 'charm', money and gifts from the thousands of [American] GI Soldiers. My new driver was gutted at the news and so to give him a bit of support I told him to get up in the turret. There was no signs of fighting and I would [take] a turn at driving – at least he could see all around and get some fresh air. All went well and finally we stopped outside this village. Sent a couple of tanks in to see what was in there, they came back and said that they had been reassured that all was safe the local people hadn't seen any enemy for over a week as they had all retreated. Great! We all got down from our tanks and started to refuel, replenish ammunition etc. and started to think about getting some food in the stew-pot whilst we had the chance. Bear in mind that I had just left the driving seat. The driver went back into his seat to get his cigarettes. He seemed to be gone a long time, so I went to tell him that the food was ready. He was still in the seat, fast asleep, or so I thought. I shouted but he didn't hear me and so I put my hand on his shoulder to rouse him. He fell forward against my arm – with a bullet hole between his eyes. It seems that there was a German sniper in a church tower that saw him moving about looking for his cigarettes. Needless to say that we pounded that village to rubble in a 15-minute barrage of shells. Rightly or wrongly, we couldn't take any more chances.

The speed of the advance meant that, at times, supplies were held up. Cliff recalls having to kill a family's pet rabbit when the emergency rations ran out.

When I hear the expression 'I'm starving' it makes me smile because not many know the real meaning of the word. Starving is when you actually feel giddy and bilious, you can't sleep at night because of the gnawing pain in your belly keeps you awake. You drink a lot of water, chew grass, dig with your hands in ploughed fields hoping to find an odd potato or swede left behind – even search dead bodies for any signs of food or a bit of chocolate.

Then I had a brilliant idea! First of all you must know that when tanks are of no more use – burned out, blown up– they are put into one big field which we called 'Tank Graveyards'. Emergency rations are carried on each tank in air-tight compartments, mainly tins of biscuits, cheese, stew and such like. So off we go to find a 'graveyard' to look for any rations that may still be there. We were lucky and found one quite quickly, raising our hopes for supper that night.

Finding the first one, I climbed to the turret, forced open the top and recoiled in horror. At first I thought that it was a little monkey looking at me from the commander's seat, then I realised that it was indeed the cindered remains of a tank commander. You can't imagine the smell (thank God he has spared you from it). I took a deep breath and tore of the ID tags from what was left of him to hand in as soon as I was able, but what upset me was the fact that this tank had been dumped without being searched properly. God Almighty! This was someone`s son, father or whoever that had been reported 'missing in action'– giving false hopes to a relative that maybe he was still alive and a prisoner of war!

After the gory find we moved on to another tank and low and behold there was 12 tins of biscuits, five tins of cheese and 15 tins of soup. You know the first thing we did? No we didn`t open up one and start eating, we just hung onto each other in one big hug and sobbed our hearts out in relief [that] we had about a week's supply if we were careful. The parting memory of that episode was that the floor of the tank was about 2–3 inches deep in burnt ashes, which I assumed were the ashes of the interior of the tank. As I pulled away to open the food locker, I felt some sort of lump beneath my hand. Pulling it free from the ashes, I looked at it and I remember screaming. It was a perfectly formed but soot-covered hand. I don't remember much else as we must have scrabbled to get back out with our food hoard wondering what else those ashes were hiding from us.'

Sometime later, having had a third tank knocked out as he commanded it in action and the death of another driver, Cliff was pulled out of the line for a period of rest until a replacement tank and crew could be found. With some medical training, he was temporarily put in charge of a half-track vehicle that was set up for recovery of the wounded and given a team of six stretcher-bearers. His job would be to go forward to help evacuate casualties for treatment.

On one of our recovery trips, we were loading up wounded and bodies of dead, when I heard the sound of tank tracks coming towards us. I new at once that it was a 'Tiger' tank – one of the most feared [German tanks]. So I started to hurry my lads up. Before we could finish loading, this Tiger tank came towards us. And didn't stop. It just went on by. We couldn't believe that we hadn't been seen on the grass verge. We started to virtually drag the wounded onto the stretchers, not being able to believe our luck! Within minutes the tank returned and again ignored us and went on around the corner.

By this time we were panicking, trying to get the loaded vehicle out from the grass verge but with all the extra weight we were having trouble to get back onto the road. Finally we did and, yes, the tank came back around the corner again (it was as if he was playing cat and mouse with us). But this time he stopped and swung right across the front of us. I recall quite clearly thinking, 'Well this is the end of the war for me' and wondered which prisoner of war camp I was going to be in.

We just stood there with our hands in the air waiting for whatever, and then the commander of this massive German tank leaned out of the top and, making a gesture of cutting his throat with two fingers, said in almost perfect English, 'Zeese ist tree times I zee you here. Four times I zee you, you are Kaput,' and drove off once again! We could not believe our luck. Needless to say, screaming wounded or not, we got the hell out of there before there was a 'four times'.

Thinking back afterwards, it wasn't so strange as it seemed for two reasons: firstly we were wearing Red Cross arm bands, were unarmed and so no threat to him; secondly, what could he have done with us? He could not have carried seven medics and six wounded on the back of his tank, could he? In retrospect, he could have shot the lot of us – it was done quite often, Red Cross or not.

Time and again in veterans' accounts come such small insights into a common humanity as soldiers struggle to survive life in the war zone with their bodies and minds intact. And then, one day, it's all over.

When this bloody war is over
Oh, how happy I will be;
When I get my civvy clothes on
No more soldiering for me.

Soldier's song of World War I

Now the bleedin' war is over
Oh how happy I was there;
Now old Fritz and I have parted,
Life's one everlasting care.
No more estaminets to sing in,
No mamoiselles to make me gay;
Civvy life's a bleedin failure,
I was happy yesterday.

Postwar variation quoted in Richard Holmes, *Firing Line*

'Soldiers may accept a need to be the first to die in a war,' wrote historian Max Hastings, 'but there is often an unseemly scramble to avoid becoming the last.' Inevitably, though, someone must be the last item on the butcher's bill. At 9.30am on the eleventh day of the eleventh month of 1918, 40-year-old Private George Edwin Ellison of the 5th Royal Irish Lancers was on the outskirts of the Belgian town of Mons scouting forward to where German soldiers had been reported in a wood. A former coal miner from Leeds, Ellison had survived the trenches for the past four years and now was back at the town where his long war had begun. In five days' time, his only son, James, would be five years old and, almost unbelievably after all he had been through, Ellison knew he would soon be going home. Already word had spread that a ceasefire would come into effect at 11am, just ninety minutes away. A single shot and he was dead, the last British soldier to die in action during the Great War.

Despite rumours of an armistice circulating for days beforehand, combat operations continued right to the very end. Aware that the war would soon be over, as the minutes ticked away Sergeant Robert Cude of 7th Battalion, The Buffs couldn't have been alone in thinking, 'If only I can last out the remainder of the time, and this is everyone's prayer. I am awfully sorry for those of our chaps who are killed this morning, and there must be a decent few of them too, for mines are still going up, and will continue to take a price from us for months to come yet.'

Marine Hubert Trotman of the Royal Marine Light Infantry was near the village of Guiry when word reached them at 9.45am. 'We were lined up on a railway bank nearby, the same railway bank the Manchesters had lined up on in 1914. They had fought at the battle of Mons in August that year. Some of us went down to a wood in a little valley and found the skeletons of some of the Manchesters still lying there. Lying there with their boots on, very still, no helmets, no rusty rifles or equipment, just their boots on'.

The graves of George Ellison and 20-year-old John Parr of the Middlesex Regiment, killed on 21 August 1914 and the first British soldier to die in the war, lie just 20 metres apart in St Symphorien Military Cemetery on the outskirts of Mons. Four years of fighting had brought the British army back to where it had started.

At 10.45am, another 40-year-old soldier, Frenchman Augustin Trebuchon, was taking a message to troops in a position on the River Meuse that soup would be served after the ceasefire. He too was killed. At 10.58am, 25-year-old Canadian Private George Lawrence Price had just entered a cottage as the Germans escaped through the back door. As he stepped back out into the street, he was shot and killed. To the south, an American private, Henry Gunther, was killed in the last 60 seconds as he attacked a German position. The Germans were aware of the ceasefire but when the Americans launched one final, futile bayonet charge they had no choice but to open fire or be killed themselves.

The decision to end at 11am was an aesthetic one. The eleventh hour of the eleventh day of the eleventh month has a ring to it that the negotiators liked but in fact, the ceasefire had been agreed hours earlier and could have been in place by dawn. The attacks that had been launched that morning were for no real purpose. Captain T.H. Westmacott noted how, shortly before the deadline, 'our Divisional Artillery let the Hun have it with every available gun. I never heard such a roar. A great contrast to the deathly silence which followed at 11am.' Gunners along the front fired off their remaining rounds to avoid having to store and return the ammunition. Conscious now that the war was over, most fired blindly into open ground, hoping to avoid killing too many of the retreating enemy. At 11am, whistles blew and, all across the Western Front, the guns fell silent.

And then it was over.

The first thing men noticed was the sudden silence. After months and years of a constant rumble of guns, men listened to birdsong and the sound of the wind. An awed hush fell across no man's land. For men who had yearned for this moment through long months of war, the first few minutes of peace brought an almost overwhelming sense of anticlimax. Lieutenant John Godfrey of the Royal Engineers remembered that 'when the news actually came, there was nothing much more than a "Thank God for that".' Some men wanted to keep going, to push the Germans back to Berlin. Some felt cheated of the chance to avenge friends and family. Some, like Archie Richards, felt that the ceasefire 'did not interest me. I had done what I had to do and just wanted to forget all about it.' Few men who were in the front line as the news came through remember any celebrations, just the calm acceptance of another order to cease fire.

There was another, widespread reaction to the end of the war – uncertainty. 'You really did just sit down and think, "What the devil am I going to do now? Job's gone,"' wrote Captain G.B. Jameson. 'Life had been so full of what you're doing, what you're planning to do, how you'd fill in your recreational time if you had any, then suddenly bang, no need for any of it, you've got to think about something else [...] You had a very fatalistic view of life. The war had gone on for so long that we really couldn't conceive that there would be any other state of affairs at all. All you thought about was survival, good luck and working your ticket home.' At the same time, Captain Charles Douie believed that the men at the front had 'learned to hold in high account some values no longer of much account in a protected country – courage, fidelity, loyalty to friends. Death was to us a byword. Our lives were forfeit and we knew it.' The sudden realisation that their lives had been handed back to them came as a shock to young men who had come to expect that the only way out of the trenches would be through their death or mutilation. Now, they had to consider a future they had barely thought possible.

Most had volunteered or been conscripted for the 'Duration of War' and now that it was over, they wanted to come home. With over seven million men in uniform, it was clear that this was going to take time. Men were allocated to demobilisation groups with each group subdivided into discharge numbers. Graham Greenwell, commissioned in 1914, considered a return to Oxford and enquired about the situation regarding students. They were, he was told, '"Class 43" on the demobilisation list – the last but one, whereas "Gentlemen" are "Class 37". So it would seem better to be a mere gentleman.' Class convention of the era dictated that first to go would be civil servants who would then administer the system, followed by those who would create jobs for others. Next came 'slip men' with chits to prove they had work to go to, followed by those with good prospects of finding work. Many men who had left work to volunteer in the heady days of 1914 were among the last to be released.

Angry riots broke out in some camps with troops waving banners declaring 'We Won the War, Give Us Our Tickets', as men who held precious employer's slips took precedence over others with longer service. At its peak, 14,000 men a day were being discharged back into civilian life. All of them worried about what the future held but all of them dreamed of the promised 'land fit for heroes' they had been told was waiting. For the older men, it would mean a return to the lives they had left behind, but more than half of the 1,859,000 troops in France when the fighting ended were 18 years old and had come of age during the war. To them it was the beginning of their adult lives and they would have to start from scratch.

During the past four years, many men had found the experience of coming home on leave difficult and uncomfortable. Gilbert Hall, for example, had struggled to find the right words when asked about life in France and in the end had given up, resorting to a few tried and tested anecdotes and the joke about a Gurkha throwing his Kukri at a German. The German called out 'Yah! You missed me', to which the Gurkha replied 'Shake your bloody head and see!' The folks at home laughed along, unable to appreciate the harsh reality underlying such humour. Elsewhere, men returning from leave spoke of alienation, of the absence of friends and the problem of finding things to talk about. After their first leave, some chose not to go home again until the war was over. Now, they would be going home for good.

Inevitably, thoughts turned to homecomings and what they would be like. 'I'll tell you what will happen to you duration soldiers,' an old sweat told Private Thomas Hope. 'You'll have the time of your lives, you'll be hugged and kissed, treated and petted, they'll have banners strung out across the streets: "Welcome Home, Our Heroic Tommies." Then some morning they'll wake up and realise the war is over, and that's when you fellows will have to start using your own toilet paper. You'll get the cold shoulder, as they'll have no more use for a penniless, out-of-work fighting man who stinks of trench manners and speech.' He was soon proved right.

By early 1919, the discharge process was rapid. Making a man into a soldier took months of training. Turning him into a civilian required only a signature. 'Ginger' Byrne of the Machine Gun Corps managed to obtain an employer's slip with the promise (unfulfilled) of a job. 'I went in to the Crystal Palace a soldier with my rifle and equipment and everything on, and I came out the other a civvy – civvy clothes, civvy suit. And I drew 35 quid blood money — that's my gratuity, see. Out of the army and out of a job.'

Even those whose employers honoured their slips had difficulty in facing the reality of their situation. One man who had left his job in 1914 returned five years later having risen to the rank of Brigadier and earned the awards of Companion of The Most Honourable Order of the Bath, Companion of The Most Distinguished Order of St Michael & St George and a Distinguished Service Order. With a glut of men seeking work after the war his employers thought they were being generous in offering him his old job back at his 1914 rate of pay.

It was the same across the country. By 1920, reports were being noted of a former Brigadier-General reduced to working as a cook for the police, and of colonels selling vegetables. George Coppard described how he 'joined the queue for jobs as messengers, window cleaners and scullions. It was a complete let down for thousands of men like me, and for some young officers too. It was a common sight in London to see ex-officers with barrel organs, refusing to earn a living as beggars [...] but there were no jobs for the "heroes" who had won the war.'

Applying for a job as a clerk, Fred Dixon was told by an interview panel that they would not be offering him a job because he had no experience. 'Why, didn't I see red! I got up on my hind legs and said, "Pardon me sir! But I've had more experience than anybody in this room, but the thing is, it's been the wrong sort! Apparently I could be fitted for war but I can't be fitted for peace. I shall know what to do another time, gentlemen!"' Elsewhere William Towers, who had lost a leg in the war, found even less sympathy as he sought work. 'He eyes me up and down, he said, "I suppose you'll have to be living on other people's generosity for the rest of your life?" I said, "Well it won't be your bloody generosity I want, goodbye!" And I walked away.'

As each man struggled to fit back into society alone, thoughts inevitably turned to the comradeship they had experienced in wartime. For many, the bonds they had formed were stronger than any they had ever experienced before or ever would again. Despite the suffering it had brought, for most men the war left a mixture of emotions. 'For my own part,' wrote Graham Greenwell, 'I have to confess that I look back on the years 1914–1918 as among the happiest I have ever spent. That they contained moments of boredom and depression, or sorrow for the loss of friends and of alarm for my personal safety, is indeed true enough. But to be perfectly fit, to live among pleasant companions, to have responsibility and a clearly defined job – these are great compensations when one is very young." In the uncertainty of the postwar world, veterans began to look back on their war as a time when all that mattered was getting through the day with the help of friends. Now, few had a purpose, no role in life and no way of communicating the complex mixture of emotions the war had created to a public that had not seen the realities of life in the trenches.

'In the years immediately following the Great War, I often heard it stated that the men who fought had no wish to talk about the War,' noted Bruce Bairnsfather, creator of the iconic Old Bill cartoons. 'Such a statement was not in accordance with fact. It is true that there was a certain reluctance on the part of ex-servicemen to discuss their experiences with people who were not in the fighting forces. This reluctance was to some extent due to diffidence and a fear that their soldier's tales might be found boring. When two or more ex-servicemen got together, however, particularly if they had been on the same front, then tongues were loosened.' Veterans found themselves able to be open with other veterans in a way they could never be with even their closest civilian friends and family.

In 1919 the King inaugurated a tradition of public commemoration and a wood-and-plaster cenotaph initially erected as a temporary measure for the Allied Victory Parade was soon replaced by an identical, permanent structure in Portland stone to act as a focus for public commemoration of the dead of the Great War. Each man who had been there, though, needed no focus. 'The day I lost my pals, 22 September 1917 – that is my Remembrance Day, not Armistice Day,' said Harry Patch, one of the last survivors of his generation. Other veterans felt the same. Throughout the 1920s, disaffected veterans protested at the Cenotaph during Remembrance Day, demanding that the country should also remember the living. The proud patriotism that had brought forward hundreds of thousands of volunteers had been replaced by bitter resentment that their sacrifice had been in vain.

Out of the public eye, across the country crime rates rose as men used the skills they had learned in war for other, less noble purposes, simply to survive. And in the years following the signing of the peace treaty, a slow trickle of men tired of the lives they felt they had lost long ago. The early 1920s were marked by the suicides of men who could not come to terms with peace and more died in a trickle in the following decades. In the spring of 1938, two girls were sitting on the banks of a reservoir near Bury when they saw a man jump from a bridge. He surfaced once, then disappeared under the water. Police with grappling hooks retrieved the body, its pockets weighted down with stones and scrap metal. Albert Forrest had served with the Lancashire Fusiliers at Gallipoli. His wife told the Coroner that Albert had come back from the war a changed man. He experienced headaches so severe that they made him cry and sat for hours just staring into the fire. On the day of his death he had apologised for the pain he had caused her and asked her to look after their son. His note, found in a bundle beside the bridge, told her, 'You have nothing to forgive, so try to forget. God bless you and Billy. I have gone off this bridge not insane, but broken hearted through my bad thoughts'. That same week, the same Coroner also dealt with the death of Henry Martin, another veteran who had been 'jumpy' since the war. His last words to his daughter were, 'It's a bad job you ever knew me.' He, too, was weighted down with stones to ensure he drowned. They weighed just 3lbs, but they were enough. Twenty-five years after the outbreak of the First World War, there were 120,000 veterans who were, or had been, receiving pensions as a result of psychiatric problems caused by their war service but they were only the ones whose problems were severe enough to make a successful claim. Then their sons were called upon to fight again in France.

For almost six years, young men who had grown up knowing how the last war had affected their fathers fought again, learning for themselves the lessons of war. At 6.30pm on 4 May 1945 an act of surrender was signed by German commanders and was due to take effect at 8am the next day. Sergeant Les Toogood was about to lead a patrol against Panzer Grenadiers. As he made ready, a messenger arrived and told him to '"Hold everything!" Oh Christ – that was better than my bloody wedding!'

As news reached the forward units, another veteran explained to historian Sean Longden that there was no emotion. 'Emotion was never shown by anybody, because if you showed emotion you were weak and it didn't go down very well. There was some drinking and shouting, but not amongst us. It was among the others, not the ones at the front. It's fair to say those who suffered the most reacted the least. Because we'd lost so much, there's no doubt we were not the same people as before. There's no way you can be the same person after something like that. So we had a different outlook on life [...] I don't think there could be celebrations because of the friends you had lost.'

'On the day the war ended,' wrote Major Peter Martin of the Cheshire Regiment, 'I felt an incredible sense of anticlimax. From the age of 19, the German war had always been there – and suddenly it disappeared. I couldn't see much point in existence any more. My whole reason for being had suddenly gone. I can remember weeping that night and I don't think I was the only person in the Division.' A feeling of somehow being singled out for survival set in for thousands of veterans. Eric 'Bill' Sykes believes that 'anyone who goes to war and survives is "Lucky". Anyone who goes to war and survives with their life and a whole body and mind is "Extremely Lucky."' Many questioned their luck, wondering why they had been allowed to survive when so many others had not.

Once again, the country prepared for the return of its men. Aware of the problems that had emerged in the 1920s, *Good Housekeeping* magazine advised American wives that 'After two or three weeks, he should be finished with talking, with oppressive remembering. If he still goes over the same stories, reveals the same emotions, you had best consult a psychiatrist. This condition is neurotic.' But two or three weeks to forget months and years of combat was hopelessly unrealistic. 'In the years immediately after the war,' wrote Sean Longden, 'in streets throughout the country, the calm of night was shattered by the screams of men reliving their experiences. By day these individuals tried to live a normal life, but once asleep the scenes of horror imprinted on their memories came flooding back. Recurring nightmares plagued their slumbers, and wives were bruised as husbands hit out violently in their sleep.' Audie Murphy, America's most decorated soldier of World War II and later a Hollywood star, slept for the rest of his life with a loaded pistol under his pillow. An advocate of the need for help for veterans, he was asked one day by a journalist about how someone gets over the type of experiences that had made him a hero. 'I don't think you ever do,' he replied.

In books, films and plays, the returning veteran was seen as a noble figure, tragically haunted by his past but unwilling to discuss what he had seen. 'Instead of talking about it,' wrote former US Marine James Jones, 'most men didn't talk about it. It was not that they didn't want to talk about it, it was that when they did, nobody understood it. It was such a different way of living, and of looking at life even, that there was no common ground for communication in it.' Like the previous generation, the men returning from World War II found it hard to readjust to the very different, seemingly petty, demands of civilian life. Bit by bit, Jones wrote, they settled back down into a humdrum existence. 'About the last thing to go was the old sense of esprit. That was the hardest thing to let go of, because there was nothing in civilian life to replace it. The love and understanding of men for men in dangerous times, and places, and situations. Just as there was nothing in civilian life that could replace the heavy, turgid, day-to-day excitement of danger. Families and other civilian types would never understand that sense of esprit, any more than they would understand the excitement of the danger. Some old-timers, a lot of them, tried to hold on to the esprit by joining division associations. But the feeling wasn't the same, and never would be the same because the motivation – the danger – was gone.' Slowly, with varying degrees of success, the returning veterans settled down to their new lives.

In both the First and Second World Wars, around one in eight of the adult male population had served in uniform. Although readjustment to life at home was difficult, there were, at least, others around who understood the feeling of alienation. After 1945, though, the military would revert to its historical role of policing a now shrinking and scattered overseas empire using small task forces. For this purpose it maintained a conscript peacetime army for the first time in British history. From 1945 until 1963, at the age of 18 young men would be called up for a compulsory two-year period.

'Although at the time of our National Service we accepted that it was a necessity,' recalls Michael Baker, who served in the Royal Tank Regiment, 'the disruption it caused at a crucial stage in our development was significant. Because I knew I would have to do National Service, I never seriously thought about what I wanted as a career, nor about going to university.' For many, National Service meant simply marking time for two years in Aldershot or on a German base before a return to civilian life.

In 1950, British troops began arriving in Korea to reinforce the United Nations contingent sent to prevent an invasion by Chinese forces. 'Very few of them knew why they were going', wrote former Second Lieutenant

Douglas John Hollands, 'and the majority of them did not care – until it was too late; they were simply doing as they were told as members of the British army.' For Jim Laird of the Black Watch, Korea was just 'a follow-on' from World War II. 'We were mystified about why someone we were fighting on the same side with during the war [the Soviet Union], an ally, was now an enemy. We were certainly very naive.'

For most, it did not matter. What mattered was surviving. Like their fathers and grandfathers, the conscripts who made up the United Nations force dug in on trench lines (this time along the dividing 38th Parallel) that would have been familiar enough to veterans of the Western Front. In the coming months, the young conscripts would face terrifying massed attacks by 'human waves', the attempts to overwhelm the defenders by sheer weight of numbers, unarmed men charging headlong at them in an effort to force them to run out of ammunition so that Chinese troops following up could destroy them at their leisure.

Yet for those who survived, there was little to distinguish them from all the other National Servicemen when it came to finding work. In his novel based on his experiences in Korea with the Duke of Wellington's Regiment, Lieutenant Hollands knew that after their five-week voyage home, their exploits would be old news. 'For a day they might be the heroes of The Hook, but they were not heroes – the heroes of the nation were a bunch of men who had climbed Everest, or sportsmen, or film stars; they were simply the latest edition of Tommy Atkins, the men who in time of peace were generally treated as the scum of the land, laughed at, sneered at, and generally held in ridicule by the public and who in time of war were taken for granted.' His men returned to find that public opinion was firmly against the war in Korea. In 1949, opinion polls had shown that 57 per cent of the public were in favour of National Service and 33 per cent against. By 1953, the figures had reversed.

More unpopular military ventures followed at Suez and throughout the remnants of the Empire as guerrilla wars against nationalist groups took a steady toll of lives in skirmishes often too small to make a story for the press at home. Men returned from these wars in batches, were discharged and went home to a country where their exploits had already been forgotten if ever truly known.

It was not until 1982 that the wider public again took an interest in the forces. The Falklands Task Force departed and returned to tumultuous crowds but, for many, it was not a joyous homecoming. For Brigadier Julian Thompson, who had led 3 Commando Brigade during the war, the homecoming was 'a marvellous experience in that it showed the appreciation of the country to the young men for what they had done, and I am glad it happened from that point of view. It was a fairly subdued personal experience for many of us. There was a feeling that we didn't want to leave the familiar surroundings of our friends, comrades and men we knew to go back to what was going to be unfamiliar. We were going among people who did not totally understand what we had done; to a world full of people who didn't know what we had gone through, who were perhaps putting the wrong connotation on what had happened, revelling in the fact of victory for the wrong reasons, as if it had been a football match, which it certainly was not. There is no fun in killing people and no fun in the actual effects of war, which are death and mutilation and terrible bereavement. I actually in some ways felt reluctant to walk off that ship among it all.'

Thompson's doubts were shared by others. As they parted for weeks of leave, returning veterans found themselves bored. 'More than anything,' wrote paratrooper Vince Bramley, 'I felt the pinch of no longer having my friends around me [...] The buddy-buddy system that we had needed to literally survive wasn't there any more and the sheltered life now seemed to me far too boring to endure. I made a point of not talking about my experiences to any member of my family, including my wife [...] Whenever I bumped into one of the lads, I seemed more at home and relaxed talking our private language with him than I did with civvies and my own family.'

Lieutenant Colonel Tim Spicer of the Scots Guards agreed. 'We simply did not want to break up the group and have to account for ourselves to our family and friends. We did not want to talk in any detail about the war and what it was like to people who had no idea of what we had been through. Naturally, our family and friends were interested and full of questions. They meant well, but they had not been there and could not understand that we did not want to talk about it. It was not a happy time, there was a lot of domestic friction, and I for one did not enjoy my leave because I could not relax. I don't suppose any of us were too easy to live with at that time, a number of marriages broke up and there was all sorts of domestic drama.'

It was hard for the families to understand. War is hell, everyone knows that. But for the veterans it was something else, too. It was fun. We are, of course, a peace-loving country, but a walk down any high street might suggest otherwise. A recent poster for a World War II re-enactment event offered the chance to 'Relive the good old days of the 1940s' in a dance that would evoke 'jitterbugs and Doodlebugs'. At weekends, civilians dress up and pretend to be soldiers, some portraying the real thing, some wearing camouflage and shooting paint at one another. Others pretend to be soldiers on computer games while still others watch war films. Yet to admit to liking war is to be seen as strange and unhealthy. For veterans who have experienced the thrill of a low-level helicopter ride or charged across the desert in a tank, who have been turned loose with heavy weaponry and been given permission to blow things up, the excitement and adventure is not a distant dream but a part of them. British photographer Tim Page, critically wounded in Vietnam, was asked by a publisher to work on a book that would '"take the glamour out of war"'. Page couldn't get over it,' wrote fellow correspondent Michael Herr. 'Take the glamour out of war! I mean how the bloody hell can you do that? I mean, you know that, it just can't be done!' Herr agreed and admitted that, for many, 'Vietnam was what we had instead of happy childhoods.'

'Our lives were forfeit,' Captain Douie wrote of the men of the Western Front. Home, mortgage, a career, household bills all mean nothing to someone who knows that they might be dead by sunset. Half a century later in Vietnam, a note placed outside a bunker at the marine base of Khe

Sanh told passers by that 'to those who fight for it, life has a meaning the sheltered never know'. For many veterans, the pettiness of civilian life became unbearable and a nostalgia set in for a time when priorities were simple and shared with like-minded others. Some veterans make journeys back to their old battlefields in part just to remind themselves of how much they once dreamed of the life they have now.

At home, though, few people expect, or want to know, about the positives. Every veteran is asked the same question: 'Did you kill anybody?' Sometimes this is asked out of lurid interest, sometimes as a challenge from those who saw the war as political and therefore the veterans as responsible for the policies that sent them to fight. It was the question every veteran came to hate. 'I got back to a surprise party with my family and the press were there,' recalls Stephen Donnell, who survived the sinking of HMS *Antelope* during the Falklands War. 'It felt weird. I didn't like it and soon got sick of all the stupid questions. "Did you kill anybody?" was about all people wanted to know.'

After trying to avoid going home when he first returned to the UK, Marine Sergeant Lou Armour stayed about a week before he hired a car and took a road trip around the country. 'I started to get feelings I wanted to tell people about. I wanted people to know about the dead people and what it's like to be shit-scared. I just wanted to get it off my chest. Instead I kept it cooped up because strangers would come up to me and say something stupid like: "Did you kill anybody?" or they'd be slapping you on the back, buying you pints, and you'd go along with it a bit. But you'd never really tell them what it was like. You'd just tell them, well, basically as much as the British public do know. At the end I had eight weeks of not telling anyone anything.'

'There is no such thing as a returning hero,' Brigadier Thompson had told his men as they returned from the Falklands, 'only returning soldiers.' As each generation returns, it withdraws into itself. It is not that veterans don't want to talk about their experiences, it's more that very few people left behind at home ever really want to hear the whole story.

And so the problems begin.

CHAPTER ELEVEN

RESETTLEMENT

Soldiers will be called upon to make personal sacrifices including the
ultimate sacrifice – in the service of the Nation. In putting the needs of
the Nation and the Army before their own, they forgo some of the rights
enjoyed by those outside the Armed Forces. In return, British soldiers
must always be able to expect fair treatment, to be valued and respected
as individuals, and that they (and their families) will be sustained and
rewarded by commensurate terms and conditions of service.

Ministry of Defence

Ever wondered why cartoon burglars all dress the same way? It's probably
not something that anyone really thinks about, but any similarity between
the dark trousers and striped jersey of the cartoon burglar and the dark
trousers and striped jerseys associated with the men of Nelson's navy is
entirely intentional. The figure that we know today first emerged in the
early nineteenth century in satirical cartoons highlighting the number of
recently redundant sailors laid off after the destruction of Napoleon's
fleet at Trafalgar who were turning to crime in civilian life.

Two centuries later, it seemed things had changed. According to a National Audit Office survey in 1997, nearly three-quarters of service leavers found the return to civilian life was as easy or even easier than they expected and only 6 per cent were reported to be still unemployed and seeking work six months after leaving the forces. Another government study in January 2010 found 2,200 veterans were in prison in England and Wales, accounting for just 3 per cent of the prison population. This, the Ministry of Defence says, makes a male veteran four times less likely to be in prison than a man from the general population. The transition back into civilian life is, it appears from these statistics, relatively simple. A ministry spokesman told reporters, 'We have a resettlement package for people leaving the forces to help them make the transition into civilian life as smoothly as possible. In 2008 the National Audit Office said the resettlement package was at the forefront of best practice.'

A study in 2010 by Colin Back, a police constable in Kent, was the first ever systematic study of the number of ex-service personnel being arrested by his force. 'I thought it would be about 30 a month coming through custody suites,' he said, 'and we got 22 in the first day.' Over a two-month period, 232 former service personnel were arrested in that one police force area alone, a third of them for violent offences. The majority were young men, mostly between 18 and 29 but some were older, up to 60 years of age. Almost 40 per cent of those detained were unemployed. Research published in 2009 by the National Association of Probation Officers suggested there were, at that time, 8,500 veterans currently in jail (about 8 per cent of the prison population) with a further 12,000 on probation or parole. Together, these 20,500 veterans amount to a number twice the size of the force serving in Afghanistan. Another study of 90 veterans on probation or parole found one in three suffered from chronic alcohol abuse while one in ten abused illegal drugs. Domestic violence accounted for a third of convictions, with other violent crime accounting for around one in five.

Harry Fletcher, assistant general secretary of the National Association of Probation Officers (NAPO), said that the optimistic figures produced by the Ministry of Defence were because their methodology was flawed. 'The MoD database lacks many first names or dates of birth and it doesn't include reservists. And since it only goes back to 1979, anyone over the age of 50, say, would be screened out.' The NAPO survey also showed that the number of veterans in prison had risen by up to 30 per cent in the preceding five years. Fletcher blames what he called 'the very macho' culture of the services that made it 'very difficult to admit that you need help […] We've got to put effort into trying to divert as many veterans as possible from being in the justice system […] It's the hidden kind of consequences of war. And I think there are things we can do to divert them away […] The root cause of much of the offending is their failure to make the transition from the highly structured, adrenalin-led military life into the community and they need help, support and counselling as a matter of urgency.'

Elfyn Llwyd MP, leader of Plaid Cymru and chair of the Justice Unions' group in the House of Commons, said of the Kent police figures that if they were 'reflective of what's going on throughout the UK, then we have a massive problem'. Veterans groups and police involved in the scheme argued that if the pattern in Kent was repeated across all 43 police forces in England and Wales, it could mean that as many as 60,000 former military personnel were being arrested annually. In fact, the figure could be an underestimate. Former military personnel, who stand to lose their pensions if convicted, could be reluctant to reveal their service record when asked in a police cell.

Lord Ramsbotham, president of the Veterans In Prison Association charity, says, 'We need to be asking, why are there so many? Because this is new, we are seeing more than before.' There should, he believes, be a standard check to establish whether an offender had previously served in the forces in order to maintain an accurate record and so that any mental health issue related to their service could be noted. 'It ought to be asked at the start and recorded in documents, particularly because of things like

PTSD [post-traumatic stress disorder]. All these factors should be presented to the judge, together with any help they may or may not have had [...] People who start off getting into trouble need someone to take them in hand and often the probation services can't give them time. It's an absolute scandal they are denied the help they need. This can start them on the road to prison.'

Harry Fletcher admits, 'There is no standardised way of identifying them in either custody suites or court reports or in prison. What does exist is dedicated individuals in the police, prison and probation service who have set up referral systems.' A veteran recalled how, when he applied for a war pension on the basis of a serious hearing loss, he was first told by the Benefits Agency that 'it was a charity job. Then, when I showed them in their own literature that I had to apply through them, the woman said it was stupid to call it a war pension when the war was so long ago! That was just four years after I got back.' Too often the word 'veteran' is misunderstood to mean 'old'.

'I was so angry when I got back,' says a former Special Forces soldier. 'I would walk into a pub, pick the biggest bloke there and go over and drink his pint and say, "OK, you got a problem with that, let's go sort it." I was just in a rage and I needed to do something with it.' For some, it is picking fights with strangers. For others, it emerges as domestic violence. Sometimes the anger turns inwards. In 1974 the American psychologist Robert Lifton wrote about the case of 'Skip' Johnson, a Vietnam veteran and Medal of Honor winner. Johnson, awarded the medal for having hunted down and killed a Vietnamese anti-tank team, found himself unable to cope with having been honoured for, as he saw it, having lost control and killing in a rage. He was killed while committing an armed robbery in New York. His mother told the press 'sometimes I wonder if he just got tired of living and wanted someone else to pull the trigger'.

In July 2009, Sir Paul Beresford, MP for Mole Valley, told the House of Commons that 'PTSD is recognised in civil life, including among police, ambulance and fire brigade personnel, among whom it has the nickname "the silent disease". The effects on sufferers can be total destruction, for them as individuals and for their families. Sufferers get nightmares and flashbacks, become hyper-vigilant, suffer panic and fear of attack, and frequently descend into alcoholism. The effects can lead to suicide. It is estimated that 262 British Falkland veterans have taken their own lives, compared with 255 lives lost in Falkland combat. Statistics released by the Ministry of Defence in March last year reveal that between 1 April 1991 and 31 December 2007, 162 British Gulf veterans died "due to intentional self-harm or from other incidents where the intent was unclear, leading to open verdicts at inquests". Veterans were, he explained, '2.13 times more likely to take their own life' than those who had never served.

'Combat veterans,' wrote psychologist John Wilson, 'are especially vulnerable to violent behaviour. If there exists an actual or perceived threat, especially to combat veterans, there is an increased probability of violent behaviour since they revert to survival skills learned in a war to cope with the threat.'

Problems arise, says Dr Claudia Herbert, director of the Oxford Stress and Trauma Centre, when military personnel leave the forces and try to fit back into normal life. 'They are running around with a body full of stored memories and, because these have not been processed, they can be triggered by what otherwise seem like everyday events. A sudden noise or movement may trigger an extreme reaction over which they have no mental control. It is a survival mechanism. Such people who have been trained to kill are dangerous, perhaps not per se, but their bodies have been trained to be killing machines.'

One of the most distressing symptoms of PTSD is hyper-vigilance – a feeling of being on a permanent state of alert. Though that can be useful when you are serving, it is a hindrance when you are trying to adjust to life as a civilian. Iraq veteran Gavin Barclay described to journalist Peter Ross how hyper-vigilance causes him to avoid a lot of life. He can't go to the pub because, when he does, he feels he has to keep his back to the wall and an eye on who is coming in. He has to be careful about going to the cinema as any sudden loud noise, especially gunfire, can make him panic; he once fled a Chinese restaurant when other diners started letting off party poppers. When he moved back in with his parents after leaving the forces, he would shout out in his sleep. "When I moved back home, I was heavily self-medicating with alcohol," he said. "I was trying to kill myself with drink … The reason I don't go out now is that the last time I did, two neds tried to jump me as I was on my way back home. The next thing I remember is a lassie screaming, "Stop it! You're kicking him in the head!" That scared me because I could have killed the guy. That's my natural instinct – if I feel threatened, I'll explode.

'Robert Lawrence, who fought and was wounded in the Falklands, said that in simplistic terms, it is like living your life with a volume switch that suddenly goes up to 20 instead of 10. You have to live at 15 in a war zone. You come back to your family, who mean much more to you than the Taliban, but they do something to piss you off and you turn the volume switch up to 20 in a world where most people never go above 10.

'When you join the army, they break you down and then rebuild you,' Barclay stated. 'They have to do that for you to become able to kill another human being. But when you leave the forces, they don't deprogramme you, so you're still that person. When I came back my family told me that I was completely changed.'

Imagine how hearing a song on the radio makes you remember something from years ago or how a smell brings things flooding back. For a while, you recall that holiday when you first heard the song or the smell of a cake baking might take you back to childhood. Now imagine how to cope if the smell of pork roasting brings images of burning human flesh. How do you explain that to a loving family?

It is only recently that Britain appointed a Minister for Veterans but, as Lord Ramsbotham points out, the post is part of the Ministry of Defence rather than at a Cabinet Office level, where it might have more influence. In the US, politicians have long been aware of the political power of the veterans' lobby but in Britain, formal groups such as the Royal British

Legion have avoided taking a political stance. But as their older members pass on, younger, more vocal veterans are taking their place. 'The hardest thing is that the treatment we got when we got home has left a lot of us very bitter. What this government needs to realise is that there's a lot of us,' says John 'Jacko' Jackson, who served with the Royal Marines. 'When you take into account all those who served in National Service and since, you're talking about a lot of people. Add in dependents and you're talking 15 million people directly or indirectly affected. This isn't 1945, we're not going to settle for three bob and a demob suit. This is the twenty-first century and we expect better. What we want is good, sound advice and information to settle back into civvy life – we learned the hard way and we want to pass on the lessons to the guys leaving so that they don't have to go through what we did.'

So what's happening to our veterans?

CHAPTER TWELVE
POST-TRAUMATIC STRESS DISORDER

PTSD

I can't go to bed,
Cause the things in my head,
Make it hard to fall asleep.

It's like it happened today,
and it won't go away.
Don't ask me to try counting sheep.

It's a part of the past,
They say the memories won't last.
Time's a great healer.

When you're lying in bed,
They can get in your head,
But only if you go to sleep.

Jim Love

When the British army went to war in 1914, its troops were ill-prepared for the nightmare ahead. Despite reports from the American Civil War 50 years earlier and the massive number of psychiatric casualties that emerged during the Russo-Japanese war at the turn of the twentieth century, few considered the possibility of mental health problems. Those who did advocated alcohol as the best treatment or, in one case, an officer of the 29th Division suggested that a minute tied to the barbed wire on the front line would cure all fear. Among the medical officers at the front were men like Charles Moran, attached to the 1st Battalion of the Royal Fusiliers and later to become, as Lord Moran, Churchill's physician and a noted authority on the morale of troops. To Moran, the men he saw were 'miserable creatures from the towns' and it came as no surprise to him that they did not appear mentally strong enough to cope with the rigours of battle. Mental breakdown was seen as a weakness of character and more likely dealt with as a disciplinary measure than as a genuine consequence of the war. Such men, if they were lucky enough to survive the often arbitrary process which distinguished 'war neuroses' from cowardice, found themselves the subjects of experimental therapies.

Among the most noted of the practitioners of extreme therapies was Lewis Yealland, a man whose fondness for using torture is recounted in Pat Barker's *Regeneration* trilogy. In one case, a 24-year-old private who had served with distinction on the Western Front and Gallipoli was struck mute. Yealland had him strapped in a chair 'while strong electricity was applied to his neck and throat; lighted cigarette ends had been applied to his tongue and hot plates placed at the back of his mouth'. Yealland argued that these failed only because they had not been applied more forcefully. Another soldier, after hours of such treatment, was told 'your laugh is most offensive to me; I dislike it very much indeed [...] You must be more rational' before Yealland turned up the voltage and started again.

Yealland was not alone. Others tried similar techniques, safe in the knowledge that the social conventions and prejudices of the day meant the men being dealt with were 'weak characters', predisposed to such hysterical behaviour and therefore malingering. As the war continued, though, the general staff were forced to reconsider. Men previously seen as steady soldiers and officers from even the best schools were also succumbing. By December 1914, only four months into the war, 10 per cent of officers and 4 per cent of other ranks were estimated to have had some sort of breakdown. Faced with what appeared to be an epidemic which could not be simply written off as a character defect, a new explanation was sought.

With a high proportion of officers among those affected, the government realised that it risked a perception that the ruling classes were rife with cowards and 'lunatics'. Whereas enlisted men became hysterical, officers were 'neurasthenic' when displaying the same symptoms. Clearly this was a common syndrome and it affected all armies. Looking to the French, British medical staff began to talk of 'shell shock'. This they divided into two categories: emotional shell shock was the result of predisposition or cowardice and unlucky cases were shot. Commotional shell shock, on the other hand, was the result of blast injuries and an honourable wound – reserved for anyone deemed to be 'a good man pushed too far'.

Although a 1922 study of shell shock concluded that there was 'an indefinite line which divides normal emotional reaction from neurosis with impairment of volitional control', belief in the predisposition of individuals was commonly held when war broke out again.

The British Expeditionary Force in France in 1939–40 was made up of a variety of units, some experienced regulars, others inexperienced territorials. Few were adequately trained or equipped and, faced with the shock tactics of the blitzkreig, the retreat towards Dunkirk was marked by extraordinary heroism but also by blind panic.

Around one-third of a million men were rescued from the beaches of France, many of whom, having watched their friends die and their regiments decimated on the beaches, broke down as they arrived at Dover. Four thousand were killed as they sought to get to the safety of the boats, another 13,000 needed immediate medical attention of whom between 10 and 15 per cent were psychiatric casualties. Anxious to avoid potentially ruinous claims for war pensions, the British government warned doctors that 'The term shell shock has been a gross and costly misnomer and should be eliminated from our nomenclature [...] No cases of psycho-neurosis or of mental breakdown, even when attributed to shell explosion or the effects thereof, should be classified as a battle casualty.'

Further military setbacks for the British followed and, with every setback came an increase in the rate of breakdown among survivors. In Malta and North Africa, the deputy director of medical services blocked the deployment of psychiatrists to the theatre and expected their role to be carried out by medical practitioners with little or no mental health training. When, after a few months, the need became obvious, two psychiatrists were deployed and were quickly swamped with work to the extent that they had to request the help of the newly arrived American forces. Even so, generals like Sir Claude Auchinlek and his replacement, Sir Harold Alexander, refused to accept the need for such help, believing that a reintroduction of the death penalty would help bolster morale.

In a conscript army, how should the 'normal' soldier react to the high probability that what he is doing will kill him very soon? How can commanders allow normal fear to exist in wartime? A 1943 study of flying stress argued that in peacetime no one would consider a coward someone who developed a fear of flying after surviving a crash that had caused the death of fellow crewmen. In wartime, however, such an attitude cannot be tolerated. All RAF aircrews were volunteers. They couldn't be treated in the same way as conscript infantrymen. Instead, anyone exhibiting signs of anxiety, fatigue or other symptoms which elsewhere might be diagnosed as shell shock or the newly termed 'battle fatigue' ran the risk of being labelled 'lacking moral fibre'. Anyone deemed to be LMF would be quickly removed from the squadron, never to be seen again by his comrades and assigned to the most menial tasks or sent to pioneer units in the army. It wasn't quite a firing squad, but it had a similar effect.

Despite the deterrent, 1942–3 saw the classification of 2,989 airmen as 'lacking moral fibre'.

As the RAF was learning about the long-term effects of its operations, the campaign in North Africa was reaching its climax. The desert war was one of high mobility and extensive operations in hostile conditions. The heat, flies, dehydration, long bombardments and frequent shifts of position all contributed to a grinding routine against a relentless threat of death. Unsurprisingly, perhaps, rates of breakdown began to climb, with up to 30 per cent of casualties being classed as psychiatric. But while the army had begun to make arrangements for the treatment of such casualties, base hospitals remained far behind the lines necessitating journeys of several days through the casualty evacuation system – far from ideal when the recognised treatment was governed by fast responses to breakdown near to the soldier's own unit in order to help speed up his return to his comrades and avoid the condition becoming too ingrained to treat.

By now, the Allies had begun to increase their efforts to study the effects of combat on those involved, since they needed all the manpower they could achieve. All these studies shared the conclusion of a US army report which declared: 'There is no such thing as "getting used to combat" [...] Each moment of combat imposes a strain so great that men will break down in direct relation to the intensity and duration of their exposure.' It even became possible to predict when that would occur. A British doctor wrote in 1942 that 'just as the average truck wears out after a certain number of miles, it appears that the infantryman wears out too. Both medical officers and line officers agreed that by the time a man had served 200 aggregate days of combat in a rifle battalion, he was non-effective. Most men, they stated, were ineffective after 180, or even 140 days. The general consensus was that a man reached his peak effectiveness in the first 90 days of combat. After this his efficiency fell away and he became steadily less valuable until finally he was useless.' During the North African campaign, psychiatric casualties ran at between 7 and 30 per cent, and another study found that after a continuous 30-day period of fighting, 98 per cent of those involved broke down. Elsewhere, against the Japanese, the 14th Indian Division was in its entirety written off as a psychiatric casualty after heavy fighting over a similar period. Among US troops in Italy, one 44-day period of fighting saw 54 per cent of casualties diagnosed as psychiatric.

The problem was one of adjustment. Paratrooper veterans of the Falklands War described the action at Wireless Ridge as more stressful than that at Goose Green because they knew what to expect in their second battle, likening it to the fear felt in the run-up to their second parachute jump – it is no longer unknown, and the mind begins to focus more on the negative aspects that you are now aware of. 'Ossie' Osbourne of the Queen's Regiment remembers how, on his first tour in Iraq, he was on foot patrol in Al Amarah. 'It was my first time on patrol there, and I have to admit to being nervous. Before we moved out, I remember the feelings I had were exactly the same as the ones I had just before I moved out of Fort Whiterock, West Belfast for the first time. Different tours, different locations, different enemy, 18 years apart but the same strong feelings of nerves and the unknown. It was strange how I recognised the feelings even with the two events being so far apart.' After a few days in combat, troops begin to adjust and filter out levels of threat and fear. After three weeks they are at their peak. By the sixth week, a 1944 report claimed, they reached what former marine James Jones describes as the 'final evolution of the soldier' – the point at which he accepts that his death is inevitable and only a matter of time. 'Every combat soldier, if he follows far enough along the path that began with his induction, must, I think, be led inexorably to that awareness […] A few men accept it immediately and at once, with a kind of feverish, self-destructive joy. The great majority of men don't want to accept it. They can accept it, though. And do accept it, if their outfit keeps going back up there long enough. The only alternative is to ask to be relieved and admit you are a coward, and that of course is against the law. They put you in prison.'

Tank gunner Joe Elkins served throughout the war in Europe in what he calls a 'never, never state', recalling; 'I quickly became a fatalist. If you didn't then you just went barmy. Luckily, my crews felt the same. I don't see any other way of keeping sane. If you thought, "I'm gonna get shot this morning," and thought, 'If I get shot, I get shot. If I don't, I don't," it becomes a fact of life. We didn't give a damn.'

On 30 June 1944 the Commanding Officer of the 6th Battalion, Duke of Wellington's Regiment wrote that they were not fit to take their place in the line. He had arrived on the evening of 26 June to find a unit that had taken 23 officer and 350 other ranks casualties in the previous two weeks and in the days following his arrival, three more officers were killed. Among the troops, he said, 75 per cent of the men 'react adversely to enemy shelling and are "jumpy". Each time men are killed or wounded a number of men become casualties through shell shock or hysteria [...] There is naturally no esprit de corps for those who are frightened (as we all are to one degree or another) to fall back on. I have twice had to stand at the end of a track and draw my revolver on retreating men.' Hearing of the report, Montgomery was furious, calling the officer 'defeatist'. The unit was disbanded, but if the experience of 6DWR was the exception rather than the rule, it was fear of this type of breakdown that forced commanders to leave the more elite units in action long after they should have been relieved.

Back in England, Northfield Hospital near Birmingham had been taken over by the military. Built in 1905 as a mental hospital, the military moved in during 1942. It was here that psychiatric casualties from Normandy were brought, 2,000 by October 1944 including 200 in a single day. Work was undertaken to rehabilitate the most entrenched reactions – those who had not responded at field hospitals and therefore were unable to return to their units as planned. Between September 1939 and July 1944, 118,000 psychiatric discharges were made, over two-thirds being 'war neuroses'. It was by far the largest discharge category.

In the years following the war, training regimes were altered to emphasise the aggression needed for combat as a result of Marshall's work. Military psychiatry developed the principle of PIE – Proximity, Immediacy, Expectancy – to facilitate the treatment of psychiatric casualties as near to the front as possible, quickly and with the expectation that they would be returned to their comrades at the earliest opportunity – a policy that remains in effect today. As a result, the number of true 'shell shock' or 'battle fatigue' cases has fallen sharply. Very few cases were actually reported in-country during the Vietnam War and the British experiences in various campaigns have all shown low rates of psychiatric casualties during operations, where the current term is 'Combat Stress Reaction' or CSR.

What was not recognised was that the long-term effects of war may not surface for some time. As the veterans of WWII reached retirement age, it became apparent that long-buried memories were rising to the surface in much the same way as those of survivors of natural or man-made disasters. As early as 1973, concerns were voiced about the readjustment problems being faced by returning veterans of the Vietnam War and the long-term implications of the emerging recognition that military service could lead to later difficulties. In the years since, extensive research has been carried out in the US and, more recently, Australia, to examine the long-term consequences of service in Vietnam on individuals and their families. This research is ongoing and has provided the backdrop for more far-reaching work on survivors of traumatic events. Bringing these findings together with those seen in survivors of the Holocaust and other man-made and natural disasters, in 1980 the American Psychiatric Association agreed a definition of a group of symptoms as a new category – post-traumatic stress disorder (PTSD). In much the same way as its wartime predecessor, and for much the same reason, the British Ministry of Defence has, for many years, chosen to downplay its existence.

Many veterans remain angry about the reluctance of the Ministry of Defence and the government to admit the potential long-term psychological consequences of military service. Instead, they have clouded the issue by discussing the low rate of CSR and encouraging the public to confuse 'shell shock' (which occurs during exposure to combat) and post-traumatic stress (which, as its name explains, affects the individual after the event). The formal recognition of PTSD in the professional literature took place two years before the Falklands War and so, veterans argue, either the MOD knew about it and chose to do nothing – making them negligent; or they didn't know about something mental health professionals worldwide had been informed of – making them incompetent.

A measure of how strongly the army attempted to resist the concept of later psychological harm came in an article for *Pennant* magazine in May 1994 when former director of Army Psychiatry, Brigadier Abraham, criticised claims by the Trauma Aftercare Trust (TACT) that over half of the troops deployed to the Gulf in 1991 developed PTSD to some degree. In fact, Abraham wrote, such a claim 'invites disbelief, discredits the very concept of PTSD and does an injustice to the nearly 200 soldiers (out of 35,000) who have in fact been diagnosed as having suffered that disorder'.

The overwhelming evidence from studies across a wide variety of veteran groups would seem to support the TACT claim, and indeed the figure was accepted by the US government about its own troops. Yet Brigadier Abraham asserted that the figure of nearer 0.6 per cent   or nearly one-hundredth of figures reported elsewhere – is accurate. Abraham's figure of 0.6 per cent may be true of CSR cases reported in the Gulf or it may be true of serving soldiers treated as inpatients at military hospitals – he does not specify how his figure was reached – but a 1991 study of Falklands veteran paratroopers identified full-blown PTSD symptoms in 22 per cent of those veterans still serving and who had not been identified by the military as experiencing problems.

PTSD is perhaps best defined as a normal human response to a death encounter. It is triggered by an event that overwhelms the body's normal defence mechanisms. Dr Claudia Herbert, director of the Oxford Stress and Trauma Centre, has worked with veterans of conflicts including Northern Ireland, the Falklands, Kosovo, Iraq and Afghanistan. She explains: 'Military personnel are trained to deal with extreme situations. They may understand the theory of how to react, but when the action occurs the reality of what they are faced with can make them react very differently. What happens in a situation of extreme trauma is that the higher order processes, the cognitive processes, tend to shut down and the body tends to predominantly operate on autonomic functioning, which is geared solely towards survival.' In response to traumatic situations, the incident is stored in the memory system of the body, the mind and the brain. 'Left unprocessed it remains a "body memory".' The part of the brain that translates feeling into communicating the experience is often shut down during trauma, so that the trauma is stored but the person cannot say what has happened to them. 'They may then experience it, relive it through "flashback", but can't actually talk about it.'

The veteran can never believe himself to be safe. People have tried to kill him. He has been a target – and perhaps still is. The feeling of insecurity is manifested through hyper-vigilance and the need to be aware of everything around him. Many Falklands veterans, for example, report being unsettled if they hear jet aircraft until they can see them – a remnant of the bombing of San Carlos. Many Ulster veterans check their cars for bombs. Some of the veterans interviewed for this book have not revealed their identity because their service has left them as potential terrorist targets.

Alongside hyper-vigilance runs a feeling of guilt. Guilt at surviving when others died and fears that in some way the veteran's performance contributed to those deaths. Alan Roberts was in Burma in World War II and took part in special operations. On one, he had to parachute from an aircraft. The last to jump, he watched as Japanese tracer rounds hit his friend and triggered the explosive detonators he was carrying. 'Your success in war isn't due to organization,' he told Caroline Freeman-Cuerden, author of *Veterans' Voices*, 'it's down to luck. If you go down one path one day you might be OK. The next day you go down the same path and you've had it. It's the one that makes the fewest mistakes who survives. I was completely ashamed and full of guilt that I felt no remorse for Geordie, only happiness that I was alive and it was him. This worried me for years and years afterwards: how could I react like that? But I've talked to other people and it's exactly the same for them – survival. Nowadays counsellors talk to everybody. With us, there was no such thing. I think counselling is wrong, it's confessions. You shouldn't take the guilt away, it should stay there within yourself. It does with me.'

PTSD may not appear for months or years after the event. In many cases, the veteran is busy attempting to settle back into civilian life and it is only later, perhaps even on retirement, that there is time to reflect. Famously, after the opening of the film *Saving Private Ryan*, many veterans found memories they had thought long-forgotten had been triggered by the film. A British Legion briefing paper reported that the triggering of wartime memories 'has been noted in Legion residential homes and appears to be an increasing tendency among residents who suffered extreme and prolonged trauma in service, for example, as prisoners-of-war. It has led to suicides and attempts at same and prompted the Legion to consider counselling for staff to enable them to anticipate this condition.'

By then, though, the veteran is someone else's problem. Dr Nigel Hunt, Associate Professor at the Institute of Work, Health and Organisations of the University of Nottingham says, 'If you start showing symptoms of war trauma during service you are the responsibility of the Ministry of Defence and you have access to a strong network of support and treatment. But many people do not develop the condition until they have left the services, once they have lost the supportive network, spending time day to day with people who understand what they have been through and how they feel. Once out of the services, they are the responsibility of the NHS, where many practitioners don't have the experience and specialist knowledge to deal with people suffering from war trauma.'

One Special Forces veteran with distinguished service in Iraq described how he eventually found himself detained under the Mental Health Act. 'I was taken to see this Asian psychiatrist. Imagine, there's an Asian guy, looking very much like the people I've been fighting, sitting behind a desk with a desk lamp shining at me. Then he starts the questions: "How many people have you killed and how do you feel about it?"' They were surprised, he says, when he decided he wasn't going to respond to interrogation. Answering questions wasn't what he was trained to do.

According to Navy Psychiatrist Commander Morgan O'Connell, who had served as the Task Force's only mental health specialist, no attempt was made to address the problem or even to consider it. Interviewed a few months after the Falklands War, O'Connell told the *Guardian* that while there had been only 16 psychiatric casualties during the conflict, in the aftermath he had already treated over a hundred. Having left the navy in frustration over the way it had treated its veterans, Dr O'Connell argues that the 'government's uncaring attitude and its policy of ignoring the fact that PTSD is affecting their soldiers is inflicting more damage on their own men than any foreign power or terrorist organisation could hope to achieve'. Unfortunately, as Dr O'Connell puts it, 'The NHS has no adequate system for treating [these] men because they usually need to be with their peer group and relate to people who understand the realities of war and service life.'

In response to this, the veterans began to turn to each other for the help they needed to come to terms with their experiences. Prison Officer Chris McPhee served in the navy in the Falklands. 'I'm normally a fairly extroverted guy, bubbly, enjoy a laugh but around [the anniversary of the war] my head just goes. I don't see anyone and I just shut down. That's why I came to the reunion – to be with the lads […] There are a lot [of Falklands veterans] in the Prison Service but there are an awful lot on the other side of the bars as well. You can't show them any favours but when they see Task Force pictures in my office there's a connection straight away – it's hard for civvies to understand but when you meet someone else who was there you just want to look after your own because that's how we survived then.'

As World War I neared its end, thoughts turned to coming home. Like their descendents, they banded together. In some towns, streets bear the names of battlefields in France and stand as a monument to the power of friendship. Veterans pooled their resources to buy land and hired other veterans to build homes for still other veterans to live in. Co-operatives started small businesses to give their old comrades a helping hand. Ex-Servicemen's Clubs sprang up where men could sit quietly over a pint and talk about the old days and help each other through the new.

Even before the last rounds were fired, a small group, mainly of well-to-do women, set up the Fellowship of Reconstruction and Welfare Bureau for Ex-Servicemen of all Ranks and all Services – quickly shortened to the Ex-Services Welfare Society. It was a typical example of the type of paternalistic charities springing up under the control of middle-class ladies to care for ex-soldiers, and had far-reaching effects. Its aims, set out in early 1919, were 'to make provision as shall be necessary for those cases of acute nervous and mental breakdown as would otherwise be sent to asylums [...] To provide or to obtain training and treatment for all cases of severe disablement.. Initially, like many similar groups, it dabbled in politics by supporting veterans standing for Parliament and campaigned against the plans to send any remaining veterans suffering mental health problems in military hospitals to what had, until very recently, been known as 'pauper lunatic asylums'. Instead, the society bought a number of properties to set up treatment centres offering nursing care, access to a psychiatrist and a chance to train in new skills at a factory in Leatherhead, Surrey.

Relations with the Ministry of Pensions were strained as the society fought individual cases for War Disablement pensions on behalf of their service users. So great was this strain that in 1938, the minister complained bitterly that, in his opinion, 'there was no need for the Ex-Services Welfare Society to exist'. At that time, the Ministry of Pensions were still making payments to 29,000 of the 60,000 accepted cases of pensionable shell shock.

After World War II, the Ex-Services Welfare Society evolved into the Ex-Services Mental Welfare Society and, more recently was relaunched as Combat Stress. It believes that 'All Veterans suffering from psychological wounds deserve access to highly specialised medical care.' Experience has shown that this is most successful where veterans are treated alongside their peers, and Combat Stress believes that members of the armed forces should be trained to recognise the symptoms of combat-related psychological injury including PTSD so that treatment may be sought quickly and rates of recovery improved.

To those ends, the society has sought to develop close relationships with serving soldiers. Following the suicide of 18-year-old Stuart Henderson while serving with 2nd Scots, the battalion adopted Combat Stress as its dedicated charity, helping to raise money and allowing serving soldiers to meet veterans suffering from PTSD, so they can listen to their stories and understand the issues at stake. Through contact with the charity's treatment centre in Scotland, it is also an opportunity for the soldiers of 2 Scots to relate their own combat experiences in Afghanistan and elsewhere, so that when the staff at Combat Stress find themselves treating an Afghan veteran, they will better understand the environment in which the problems developed.

'The army has always had a very male, macho culture,' says Clive Fairweather, a former deputy commander of the SAS and chief fundraiser for Combat Stress in Scotland. 'They don't want to talk about these problems and these issues. But that's beginning to change. It's a trickle that's become a swell. Civilian life has become more accepting of mental health problems and that has percolated through to the army – particularly an army that has been involved in two major conflicts in recent times.' Lieutenant Colonel Nick Borton, commanding officer of 2 Scots, agrees. 'Everyone is now much clearer on what the problems are,' he says. 'Combat Stress are currently dealing with guys who served in the Falklands, Northern Ireland and Bosnia, but everyone is very conscious that we're fighting the most intense conflict we have done for many years, and we are aware that, downstream, there are going to be people who have difficulties as a result.'

Combat Stress treats veterans in different ways, using relaxation techniques, cognitive behavioural therapy and eye movement desensitisation reprocessing, which attempts to 'reprogramme' traumatic memories through intensive therapy. Perhaps its most important contribution to the lives of veterans is the sense of community: although the staff are mostly civilian, the men and women treated there are all military veterans, and are often there for two weeks at a time. They provide a support network for each other that can be difficult to find in the civilian world, creating, as one veteran describes it, a feeling of 'walking straight back into the barracks'. That meant that when soldiers from 2 Scots visited the Hollybush Centre, 'They just sat down and were able to relate to these people, and the veterans were able to talk through their experiences without having to explain what this acronym means or that abbreviation means,' says Major James Loudoun, 2 Scots' officer commanding charities and a Scottish ambassador for Combat Stress. 'When somebody says I was bugging out towards the RV, my soldiers are able to say, "Yep, I know exactly what you mean." I think it was pretty good therapy for the soldiers to understand the help that is available and see it's not *One Flew Over the Cuckoo's Nest* – it's a proper facility where you can come and get help, meet people who understand, and then get on with your life.'

Major Loudoun visited Hollybush with two colleagues to discuss with the nursing staff the conditions men and women are facing on the front line in Afghanistan. 'We took the opportunity to say, "Look, this is what's happening here and now. You'll get soldiers talking about the living conditions and the shooting and the heat and we can tell you more about that." We took along props so they understood the weight of what we were carrying, the size of the area we lived in, the harshness of the environment, the food, to highlight the stress that soldiers are under so that in the future, they'll be able to understand where soldiers talking about Afghanistan are coming from.'

Most veterans, of course, never need the intensive support provided by Combat Stress treatment centres. Most cope, one way or another. Anniversaries of battles or of friends' deaths are always a bad time. November with its remembrance theme is mixed with the explosions of fireworks in the streets and that's often when the veterans withdraw. Many years ago, living in Brighton, I left my house one day after there had been a firework spectacular to celebrate the completion of work on the new marina. An elderly neighbour knew I had been in the forces and stopped for a chat. We talked about the display. He hadn't slept that night. 'I was in Norway in 1940,' he said quietly. 'Brings it all back...' I nodded. I knew what he meant.

Stephen Donnell is typical. 'After I left in 1985 I couldn't settle and drifted from job to job until I joined the Prison Service in '91. I wanted to come to [the reunion] to meet people who had had the same experiences, been part of the same history. I don't think I've suffered PTSD like some of the lads [...] no, scrub that, I think it affected everybody in one way or another, I've just been lucky.'

Scott was twenty years old when, in 1990, he was posted to West Belfast. He remembers:

'The atmosphere was intense. One Sunday night I was on a routine patrol, travelling in an armoured Land Rover towards a potential hotspot. We were just two minutes outside camp when I saw a flash of white light – and realised a split second later that we'd been hit by a rocket propelled grenade. More than anything, I was just glad to be alive.

At the time, it didn't really affect me: I was in an army environment and you didn't have time to ponder it. It was only after I left the Services that I realised I wasn't the same person. By my mid-twenties I started to get flashbacks to the explosion – weekly, daily, eventually hourly. For nine months I barely slept, and when I did, I had nightmares. My mind became hellish. And so in February 1999 I took a massive overdose. I just wanted the pain in my head to stop.'

Later that year I made my first visit to Hollybush House in Ayrshire.

The first few years were a real struggle – no denying it – but two treatments made all the difference to me: EMDR [eye movement desensitisation and reprogramming] and CBT [cognitive behaviour therapy]. Thanks to EMDR, I don't have flashbacks any more. CBT taught me to take little risks, one step at a time, to re-establish myself in the world. After nine years out of work, I'm now a postman in the Highlands. And I'm starting to enjoy life. I wouldn't have managed it without Hollybush. The staff gave me the techniques and coping mechanisms to move forward.'

For Hugh, the bomb disposal expert threatened by a gunman in Bosnia, life after the army was difficult. Medically discharged from the forces, his marriage broke down and he lost his job after breaking his boss's fingers in a wage dispute. Eventually, he too attempted suicide. He was finally diagnosed as suffering PTSD and referred to Combat Stress. '[That] saved me from killing myself,' he says. 'Life is not perfect, but the therapy has taught me how to minimise the flashbacks. When things get too much, I'm now very good at saying to myself, "You're in a house in Essex, you are not in Bosnia".'

Julie enlisted in the Royal Logistic Corps as part of Expeditionary Forces Institute, the uniformed equivalent of the NAAFI that provides facilities to frontline troops. In 1997, she was sent to Bosnia for the first time and returned in 1998 and again in 1999 for a two year posting.

Sent out to work as a shopkeeper, she once had to mount guard on a mass grave and to clear the blood from the site of a grenade explosion that had killed a soldier and civilians. In 2002, she found herself posted to Afghanistan.

' Death was everywhere,' she recalls, 'the result of bombings and shootings. The threat and danger was intense. Most things were done at night for safety. Just driving off camp, you always potentially had a price on your head.' By now, her years of operational duties were taking their toll. 'I was having nightmares and losing confidence in myself. I had a permanent 'fed-up' feeling and I asked to be replaced. A CPN

(Community Psychiatric Nurse) recommended a week's leave to the UK. On the long flight back I was charged with guarding the remains of two dead soldiers – one of whom was a friend.

'When I returned to Afghanistan there was a notable change in my behaviour and my work was failing, so I was called in to see a CPN. A doctor then had me flown out to Catterick. Within a week I was discharged from the army, in September 2002. It took a long time to sink in. I was told I had an adjustment disorder and that in six to twelve weeks I'd be back to normal. I waited for the twelve weeks to end, but they never did. I spent three years like that – not working, not going out of the house, not getting up some days. I had nightmares, panic attacks and flashbacks. In 2005, the Social Services put me on to the Veterans' Agency, and in 2006 I was awarded a 40% War Pension following a diagnosis of post-traumatic stress disorder. It was the Veterans' Agency who told me about Combat Stress. My first admission to Audley Court in Shropshire was in September 2006. I didn't want to go at first – I had to force myself because I knew I needed help. At the end of that week I didn't want to go home. I felt safe for the first time since before leaving the Army. This is my fourth visit.'

For all the veterans using Combat Stress, there is an almost palpable sense of relief that they are able to talk about their experiences in an environment in which people want to understand and where the veterans don't feel judged. 'They talk about survivor guilt,' one Falklands veteran recalls. 'I remember seeing a civilian therapist who told me it was right that veterans should feel guilty because of what we did to the Belgrano. Another NHS staff member told me I must be a Thatcher supporter because I'd "fought her war for her". Then, when you clam up because you feel you can't talk to these people, they can discharge you and it's all your fault for being in denial!'

Subject to the Official Secrets Act and having taken part in operations that may be classified or politically controversial, many veterans feel constrained in what they are able to discuss and frequently judged for their behaviour by people who have no concept of what combat entails. Finally reaching Combat Stress allows them to meet with people who do know and who don't judge. 'The nightmares are still there,' says Julie, 'though less frequent. And I still have panic attacks. But if my life never improves from now, I know I can cope – whereas before I couldn't even see the next day, never mind the future. I wouldn't be here if it wasn't for this place. I know I wouldn't – but I am.'

'Still now', says Gulf veteran James Saunders, 'I can't talk to civvies about it because you're just going to see a blank expression on their faces. They just can't comprehend or understand, that's the long and short of it. You can see in their eyes they have no comprehension of what you're talking about. It's not until you talk to a military guy, it seems that's when you find a commonality'.

As a Lance Bombardier in the Royal Artillery during the first Gulf War, he experienced a "friendly fire" incident in which his unit came under attack by British Challenger tanks and later 'there were the sights of the Basra road and images of the burning oilfields. In hindsight, at the time they didn't affect me. There were no problems while I was actually in the theatre of operations. It was after my return where signs and cracks started to appear.' After a six-month tour of duty he came back to the UK and requested leave so he could attend the birth of his child, but was refused permission. Instead, he went AWOL.

"Tragically my son died at birth, which kick-started all my PTSD problems and other associated disorders that go with it,' he recalls. On his return to the army he was sentenced to imprisonment at the Military Correction Centre and, when he rejoined the artillery, 'they put me in HQ, which is basically an administration unit. So I wasn't really a frontline soldier anymore, and that sent me into a spiral of depression and I really lost total interest in my army career after that point.' From then on, until his army career ended in 1993, service was 'like a long train ride until it crashed at the end'.

'I kept getting worse depression, I left the army, still dealing with the death of my son and got involved in drink and drugs,' he says. 'My tangle with alcohol and drugs just got worse and worse and where drugs were involved it eventually ended up with me going to prison.'

'That was almost the starting point for my recovery. It was from that point then that I actually started to seek help. I realised there was something seriously, seriously wrong and if I didn't get a grip on it, it was going to spiral out of even more control.' The problem was that the prison system was unable to provide it. 'I was asking people – doctors, nurses – and no one could help me,' says Saunders. 'I was either told they weren't experienced or didn't have the ability to deal with my sort of case.' When he was released, he found it difficult to find any practical support through the NHS and felt his life was sliding towards disaster until a friend referred him to Combat Stress.

He describes his first visit to the Tyrwhitt House treatment centre as a revelation and found support that matched his treatment and therapy to his own personal goals. 'There's not just one cure, there are many symptoms that go with this,' he says. 'Once you've been assessed they tailor your treatment and think what the best route for you is as an individual. They provide the correct treatment at the right time in the right place. They give you a safe environment to be in, away from everyday life, where you can actually address the problems and get the correct treatment tailored to your specific needs. They really do know what they're doing and make a hell of a difference to a lot of people.'

In the fourteen years between Saunders' tour in the Gulf and his referral to Combat Stress, he had survived self-destructive behaviour that had left him feeling out of control. 'I had no fear about anything, no self control over my temper,' he says, 'I had extremely aggressive outbursts, night sweats, sleep deprivation, a whole catalogue of other symptoms as well, including depression. These aren't just on a daily basis; some of these things can last for weeks and months.' James was 21 when he went to war and today, five years after he began receiving help, he says he is finally in 'a good place' mentally and is working towards his dream of a career as a sound engineer and photographer. He puts his state of mind entirely down to the help he has received from Combat Stress. 'That's where my recovery began,' he says. 'Literally as soon as I walked through the door.'

CHAPTER THIRTEEN
LAST POST

When the hurly-burly's done,
When the battle's lost and won.

William Shakespeare, *Macbeth*

For those who survive, what does courage under fire mean? To most it means simply doing what you are paid to do. 'Soldiers have always died on ops,' one veteran explains. 'Bullets and bombs have a tendency to kill and maim soldiers. Even if casualty rates were actually higher in Afghanistan than in World War II we'd still have to go out there and crack on. That's what we get paid for; doing our job. Whether we don't like it or don't agree with it is irrelevant.'

At the age of 14, Charlotte Madison was sent to boarding school in England, where she joined the Combined Cadet Force (CCF) because that's where all the hot boys were. She loved the camaraderie of the CCF and stuck with it through school and university. It was only in her second year of reading civil engineering that she realised, she says flippantly, that she 'didn't have many other useful talents'.

After taking a short course, she was granted a temporary gap year commission before taking up her university place. It was during a summer field exercise in Canada that she first had the opportunity to fly in a helicopter and from that moment was hooked. At 21 she went to Sandhurst, and finally achieved her ambition to join the Army Air Corps. The only combat arm to allow women to work on an equal basis with men in battle, she worked hard to become the first woman accepted into the intensive training course for the AH 64 Apache attack helicopter. As the sole woman on the course she was on her own, and it came as a shock: always comfortable around men, she'd assumed she wouldn't miss female company. In reality, she found herself cornering cleaners in corridors, desperate for female conversation, preferably banal. The men didn't help themselves. They waved Yorkie-style stickers around that read 'Apache – it's not for girls'. Some, she thinks, willed her to fail because she was female. She took to eating dinner in her room because she couldn't stomach any more 'willy-waving' competitions.

'That [killer instinct] was seamlessly trained into me,' Madison said later. 'I dunno what I'd call it. Being professional at the job, I guess, but that sounds a bit wrong.' She spent so many hours in simulators and on training sorties, firing fake weapons at fake targets, that when she finally went to war it simply felt like an extension of that. 'It just felt like I was in the simulator. We were chasing the enemy. We circled, we tracked some movement. All you want at that moment is to protect the guys in the patrol base. It's almost maternal. It was just like a drill. I was really proud of myself that it wasn't a big thing for me. I didn't whoop or have a wave of emotion, thinking that I couldn't do it because it was so hideous. I was just doing what I was supposed to be doing [...] I didn't even think about my first real engagement with real people and real weapons until we were flying back. My backseater said, "Was that your first one?" and I thought, "Oh my goodness, yes it was." I honestly [...] felt nothing. It wasn't like I was [she puts on a gung-ho voice], "Yeah, I'm really happy, I went and killed loads of people." I felt really happy that I'd done my job. If there are Taliban in a building and one of the guys on the ground says, "Can you destroy it?", yes, we can, with a missile. And it'll be completely taken care of.'

Like all aircrew, Madison was interviewed after every flight. 'They say, "What did you shoot that for? How many rounds did you use? Did you need that many?" Everything is very measured. It's not like we're all just ruthless killers going out.

'I'll do whatever the soldiers on the ground need,' she continues. 'I'm not going to question it first. They're in danger and they need someone who can identify good from bad. So I do see it as life-saving.' With each tour, she found herself increasingly affected by the missions. 'I became more sensitised to it. The more bodies that came back, the more you start thinking this is horrible. You start questioning yourself that little extra bit.'

Although the army does not regard the Army Air Corps as engaging the enemy 'face to face' (the term used to define those roles barred to women in other units), the close-in support they provide and the gun cameras onboard to record every engagement make it impossible for Apache crews not to be fully aware of the effects of their weapons on the men they target. In her book *Dressed to Kill*, Madison described how the stress of daily attacks on Taliban positions began to take a toll:

'I don't know what makes a normal topic of conversation any more,' I tell Jo, another female British Apache pilot who has joined us in Afghanistan.

'Something has been playing on my mind, too. Some of the boys keep a "kill count". I don't, but I have an idea of the scale of what I've done. You know,' I say slowly, wanting to gauge her reaction, 'I've killed more people than Harold Shipman, Myra Hindley, Jack The Ripper and any other serial killer you can name all put together. If that's not f*cked up, I don't know what is.'

I want to see if she looks horrified.

She looks me straight in the eye. 'I think of our job as being like an airborne hitman. You get a scrap of paper with a grid on it and get told to kill whoever's there. It's kind of cool. And we're on the side of good.'

Now this is the difference, I think to myself: this is her first time out here and my last. I used to think it was cool.

I was always so satisfied with myself when a mission went well, when I could see the gun tape of me shooting the bad guys. But now I'm not so sure. I know we're supposed to be on the right side, but that's what those guys think too. And they have mothers, and kids …

I stop, not wanting to go down that road.

Madison left the army in December 2009, aged 29. She says she wants to spend time with her husband, who she thinks will stay in the forces indefinitely, and doesn't believe having children is, for her at least, compatible with active service. She wants to carry on flying, maybe an air ambulance, but it's still early days. Looking back, she explains:

The first thing that springs into my mind when someone says 'courage under fire' is the stereotypical image of WWI soldiers going 'over the top' from the trenches; the key aspects being knowing what they were about to face and that it was very dangerous, and doing it anyway. Certainly the phrase doesn't immediately bring to mind anything I have done. But if courage under fire is being able to do your job professionally while someone is trying to kill you, then many of my missions in Afghanistan certainly fit the bill.

I am frequently asked 'Were you ever scared?' and the honest answer is that of course I was, but never in the situations people are imagining. I was frightened when I was fighting an 80mph wind and thought I was going to get blown over the Iranian border, I was scared when my night vision system failed and I thought we were going to hit another aircraft, but I genuinely never had that same adrenalin rush of 'I think I'm going to die' because I was being shot at. Maybe I'm too stupid, but I actually think it is because of two factors.

Firstly, you need an incredible amount of focus to do any job on the front line. The margins for error are tiny: Apache pilots are firing our 30mm cannons within tens of metres of British troops to try and protect them and it only takes a tiny twitch of your finger to make a fatal mistake; that's a risk we can't take. And when you are tracking an enemy fighter who has perhaps just killed a British soldier you might only get a tiny flash of him as he darts through a treeline to try and identify him; you can't afford to miss that opportunity or get it wrong. This single-minded focus pushes everything else out of your mind, and I have frequently replied to a radio call letting me know I'm being shot at with an automatic 'Roger' because it seems irrelevant in the face of the task in hand.

Secondly, you never know how bad it was or how close you came to dying until afterwards. I have received countless radio calls from my wingman saying 'RPG [rocket propelled grenade] just missed you' and sent many similar radio calls back. I have watched slow motion gun tape footage of RPGs crossing in all directions just metres in front of my aircraft, and handheld camera footage of airburst ammunition peppering the sky in a ring around my helicopter. That's when you get the delayed clammy, sweaty feeling of 'Did I do something stupid today? Did I nearly kill myself?' But by then it's all over, and next time you go flying you do the same thing again.

The other aspect of all this, and in my mind the most important, is one that is almost impossible to describe to someone who hasn't been in the forces. The closeness that develops between a team fighting together on the front line is second to nothing. When people ask me whether I think that most soldiers believe the war in Afghanistan is the right thing, I tell them it doesn't matter. Each soldier is fighting for the others in his team; for the man standing

beside him, for his best mate who has just been injured, for the rest
of his fire team who are relying on him.

In the air it is no different. You get to know the voices of the
soldiers in the various Forward Operating Bases and speak with
them every day. The frightened voice of one of these soldiers on the
radio, asking for your help with the sound of gunfire in the
background, focuses every nerve in your body. I have also been lucky
enough to fly with, in my opinion, some of the most capable and
professional pilots in the Army Air Corps and that is something that
was also constantly on my mind – you are both strapped onto the
same piece of metal thousands of feet in the air with someone trying
to kill you and no way to get out, and don't want to let them down
by screwing up. And when you work together closely with someone
you trust, who trusts you, it can make you feel almost invincible.

Everyone I know who has returned from Afghanistan has come
back a changed person, and I am no different. I have nightmares
about being killed, I trust myself more and less at the same time and
my whole perspective has changed.

I trust myself more because I know that when the time came for
me to face my biggest challenges, I was up to the task – of course I
made plenty of mistakes, but none that were big enough that I can't
live with them.

I trust myself less because I don't feel at all like the same person
who was in Afghanistan a year ago. I can't believe I was able to go
through the things that I did and face up to so many fears and
uncertainties at once. The fact that I was able to, I put solely down to
the incredibly brave and competent people I was lucky enough to
serve with – the respect I have for them is total and if they trusted
me I was able to trust myself. I haven't yet decided whether I'm a
better or a worse person as a result of the things I was asked to do; I
think that will only come with time.

My perspective has totally changed, although it is amazing how quickly humans can adapt to different situations. When I returned from my first operational tour in Iraq, I was barely able to go to Tesco – the choice was too overwhelming and I couldn't bear hearing people complaining about such-and-such an item being out of stock when all I wanted to do was shout 'Don't you know there's a war going on? Do you know how lucky you are to only be worried about bread?' A year after my final tour, of course I am back to worrying about small things like whether there is damp in my kitchen wall, but I am able to step back and know what is genuinely important in my life.

The single thing that has affected me most on returning from my time in Iraq and Afghanistan is that people generally have no idea what our armed forces are asked to do for us. If I could change one thing about the way people view the forces, I would ask that when there is something on the news, or in the papers about Afghanistan, they take a minute to consider what life is like for the thousands of teenaged boys living in hostile conditions with no fresh food, no sanitation and nowhere safe where they can sleep. Consider that they haven't chosen to be there, they are just doing the best they can with what the government has chosen for them.

While I'm sure everyone in the country would rather there was no need for global conflict, I would ask people to be grateful that there are young volunteers willing to risk their lives for the security of the rest of us at home while we go about our daily lives, unaware of what is going on right this second in war zones around the world.

David 'Mog' Morgan won the Distinguished Service Cross as a Sea Harrier pilot during the Falklands War. In the years that followed, he began to suffer the effects of post-traumatic stress and found that writing about his experiences through his book *Hostile Skies* and his poetry were, he says, 'enormously therapeutic' for him. His poem 'They were but men ...' earned him national recognition and remains widely known. But in the dark days of PTSD he wrote more private verse:

NIGHT RETURNS

Black night returns;
Its icy fingers clawing at my vital heart.
Great loneliness engulfs my soul
And truth and beauty flee once more
My wretched breast.

Where once was life
And love unbounded, lies but dark
Dread and pain, with evil worms
That gnaw and wriggle in my gut
And freeze my brain.

My day is done.
There can be nothing more beyond this hell.
No golden dawn to wrench me back to life,
No final trump to slow and halt
My downward slide.

David Morgan

Recovery took time but in 1992 he left the RAF and took a job with Virgin Airways. Today he divides his time between flying 747s on long-haul flights and a Yak 50 for the Yakovlev aerobatic display team. Looking back at his experiences, how does he feel about being what many would see as a war hero?

'I think that if you talk to anyone who has been "courageous" under fire, they will tell you that it wasn't a conscious decision but a combination of training and adrenalin. Very few people decide to be brave, they just react to the situation. The people who demonstrate real bravery are those who are scared shitless but go out and do the job in spite of that.

'To a large degree, the award of medals is down to luck. Luck to find yourself in the situation and luck to be nominated! Having said that, you can generate your own luck to certain extent. As someone once said, "The harder I work at it, the luckier I get."

'Without doubt, stamina, personality and determination play a part but I feel that training is the most important factor. The closer to reality you can make your training, the better you will fight. I really dislike the term "hero". I have never personally come across anyone who qualifies for that epithet and it is bandied about far too readily by the press. Servicemen who die are not heroes. They are doing their job to the best of their ability and luck out.

'To a large extent, the real fight comes after the battle is over and the adrenalin dies down. Re-adapting to civilian life can be extremely traumatic for those who cannot close their eyes, or hear a loud bang without reliving the trauma of conflict. That is where real bravery comes in; forcing yourself to get up and face the world on a daily basis, fighting off the waves of black despair and trying to keep your life from sliding into alcoholism, violence or self-harm. I was lucky enough to have the support I needed to pull through and regain my equilibrium but others are not so lucky.'

'I yam what I yam,' said Private Kenny Bosch, echoing Popeye. It's a good analysis of the soldier. On the subject of courage under fire, Captain Sam Drennan, whose evacuation of Robert Lawrence from Tumbledown earned him a Distinguished Flying Cross, told historian Max Arthur, 'I think we all hope that when it comes to the test that we're going to find reserves of whatever is required. As military people, we train for war, and hope it never comes, but we train for it seriously. I think we all have this nagging doubt in the back of our minds that when it comes to the crunch, when our life's on the line, are we going to be shrinking violets or are we going to find the depths of courage required to do our jobs, and do them properly? That is something that has always been at the back of my mind, and I'm relieved that I've actually been put to the test and passed. I'm sure nearly everyone passed as well. I don't want to do it again, but I've looked inside myself to see what was there and I wasn't too ashamed of what I found. I can look at myself in the morning, when I'm having a shave, and not feel guilty.'

And it is in the morning, when shaving, that Borneo veteran Keith Scott remembers who he once was:

I was a soldier once, and my business was with certain sections of humanity at the sharp end, aftermath, and 'fallout' of military conflict with all that it entails. As I dragged that out of the silence of my thoughts and into a world of sound and vision, the steam on the surface of the mirror dried and the face of the man in jungle green withdrew. The glass was now empty and the quick had left the silver. It was as if I saw a figure resolving into a charged and meaningful day of cloud and thunder and lightning, and then the monsoon rains in Borneo. All I owed that young man now was a decent farewell and a proper thank you, and I found myself doing it the way that the native peoples of Borneo do it […] They call after the vanishing person, 'We see you, we hear you, we know you, we praise you, and we thank you.' These calls can and do continue long after the traveller has disappeared into the landscape. Experiences like this tend to colour your thinking for the rest of your life. I hope though, I shan't always be a traveller. All I ever wanted out of life was a quiet and peaceful heart, wherever I was living. It is just that I've never really minded where that is.

Considering where I was at that point in my life, together with what I experienced and saw, Malaysia would have been a good choice. But this journey of the mind and of the heart is not yet complete. I owe that young man much, as well as the people and organisation that trained him, not so much because of what I once might have wanted for myself, or where I am now, but who I am now. So to him and the others involved I say, 'I see you, I hear you, I know you, I praise you, and I thank you.'

ACKNOWLEDGEMENTS

It is perhaps a measure of the recognition among veterans of the work done by Combat Stress that so many were willing to help in providing material for this book and all provided their help freely and willingly. Space does not permit a personal thanks to all but I would particularly like to express my appreciation of the generosity shown by ex-Para and former Foreign Legionnaire Jim Love, whose work deserves a wide audience. His poems and stories can be accessed at www.postpoems.com and at www.britains-smallwars.com/Jim-Love/intro.htm. Thanks too, to James Paul at the excellent online resource for anyone interested in British military history since 1945, www.britains-smallwars.com for his help in contacting veterans and obtaining permission to quote from their accounts. Staff at www.wartimememories.co.uk were equally willing to share the fruits of their labour in a good cause, as was Ken Wharton, whose own series of books on the army's experiences in Northern Ireland are vital to an understanding of what happened there.

Charlotte Madison and David Morgan were both quick to respond to my e-mails and immediately gave permission to use any material I wished from their own published accounts (*Dressed to Kill* and *Hostile Skies* respectively). Each then sat down and produced their own contributions to this book and I am deeply grateful for their honesty and openness.

Audrey Gillan, Special Correspondent for the *Guardian*, gave me free access to her archive of material covering a wide variety of stories linked to the experiences of veterans at www.audreygillan.com and her account of Garmsir forms an important part of this book.

For anyone who served in the British army since the 1970s, Harvey Andrews' song 'The Soldier' has a special place in the heart. When I approached him for permission to use it in this book, he did not hesitate to agree and to work with Bob Harris at Westminster Music Ltd to make it possible for it to be used free of charge.

The book would not have been produced without Mark Searle at Elliott and Thompson and Robert Marsh at Combat Stress. Both trusted me to get on with it without interference from either. That allowed me to concentrate on making the book an honest account of the lives of our veterans.

My own family have contributed the most to getting this finished. My wife Jacqueline has worked tirelessly to allow me to work without the routine distractions that so often get in the way despite having more than enough to do herself. My daughter Bethany has been patient about my absences and my son Joshua has been ... well, he's six. Let's just say he is the leaves on the line to my train of thought – but sometimes you need to be reminded that there's more to life than writing.

Finally, my gratitude and respect goes out to Tommy (and Tammy) Atkins, to the Ruperts and the Rodneys who, wherever, whenever, do their job. Safe home at Endex guys.

They fight our wars. We fight their battles.

ABOUT COMBAT STRESS

Combat Stress was founded in May 1919, just after the First World War.
Our original name was the Ex-Servicemen's Welfare Society and we
opened our first recuperative home in 1920 on Putney Hill in south
west London.

The charity was ahead of its time. The prevailing attitude to mental
welfare was, by today's standards, primitive, even barbaric.

Those who suffered from mental breakdown during their Service life
received little or no sympathy. Indeed, during the First World War, if it
led to a failure to obey orders, death by firing squad was always
a possibility.

At the end of the war there were thousands of men returning from the
front and from sea suffering from shell shock. Many were confined in
Mental War Hospitals under Martial Law – with the risk of being sent on,
without appeal, to asylums.

But the founding mothers of Combat Stress (they were mainly women)
believed that these men could be helped to cope with their condition
through a rehabilitation programme.

Work was seen as essential to masculine identity; it provided men with financial security and many doctors believed it to be an excellent form of therapy. So, for many years, Combat Stress ran employment schemes that created real work opportunities for Veterans.

Much has changed since then. With a current caseload of more than 4,400 Veterans, we have never been busier.

In March 2010 our Patron HRH The Prince of Wales launched 'The Enemy Within Appeal' on our behalf. This £30 million, three-year fundraising campaign will enable us to:

- Establish 14 Community Outreach Teams nationwide – bringing clinical care and welfare support to Veterans in their local areas.
- Enhance clinical care at our three short-stay treatment centres, in Ayrshire, Shropshire and Surrey.

Please support our work in whatever way you can. Thank you.